THE

WAY

OF THE

KINGDOM

THE
WAY
OF THE
KINGDOM

Exploring God's Original Design

ROBERT COCHRAN SMITH JR. M.TH.

TATE PUBLISHING
AND **ENTERPRISES**, LLC

Published by Tate Publishing & Enterprises, LLC
127 E. Trade Center Terrace | Mustang, Oklahoma 73064 USA
1.888.361.9473 | www.tatepublishing.com

Tate Publishing is committed to excellence in the publishing industry. The company reflects the philosophy established by the founders, based on Psalm 68:11,
"The Lord gave the word and great was the company of those who published it."

Book design copyright © 2013 by Tate Publishing, LLC. All rights reserved.
Cover design by Samson Lim
Interior design by Mary Jean Archival

Published in the United States of America

ISBN: 978-1-62510-276-8
1. Religion / General
2. Religion / Christianity / General
13.03.12

Dedication

This book is dedicated to

My dad, Robert C. Smith Sr.,
who trained me to put the kingdom first

My mom, Jennie, who taught me
how to live by the Word

Contents

Introduction

"Your kingdom come, your will be done." In order to even *want* to pray this prayer, we must have an idea of what we are asking for. In the minds of most people today, the kingdom of God is inconceivable. We find ourselves separated from the story of creation by over six thousand years and unable to even *imagine* what an eternal future with God looks like, and then, we find a scriptural directive to pray for God's kingdom to come and his will to be done. Most people are not going to diligently ask for something that they do not understand. In order to desire the kingdom of God in such a way that compels us to pray for it, we must first see it with the eyes of imagination, become acquainted with the plan of God, and find out what motivates him to carry it out. I am convinced that the way of the kingdom is reserved for the ones who are willing to search it out.

The Law of the Kingdom

The common idea of law, and the mental images that are generally conjured up, are usually anything but positive. The practical definition of *law* is "that which confines, limits, or restricts freedom, and those things that one is compelled to do in order to be found in good standing." Some are convinced that laws are made to keep a person from having fun and adventure. After all, there are many exciting and pleasurable things that are also illegal, right? The grass is always greener on the other side, forbidden fruit always tastes sweeter, rules are made to be broken, I just wanna be free—sounds familiar doesn't it?

Our modern society is groaning under a law system that is oppressive and seemingly void of intelligence, but the law of God's kingdom does not even resemble the common concept of law. It stands at a different viewpoint and exists for a completely different purpose.

The primary word in the Greek New Testament for law is *nomos*, which means "to parcel out, either by distributing or assigning—because the law assigns to everyone his own—or of administering because it administers all things either by commanding or forbidding." So in essence, law defines your portion and allotment and, therefore, your life. The focus of kingdom law is primarily on everything you *can* have and *can* do.

> Then God blessed them, and God said to them, "Be fruitful and multiply; fill the earth and subdue it; have dominion over the fish of the sea, over the birds of the air, and over every living thing that moves on the earth." And God said, "See, I have given you every herb that yields seed which is on the face of all the earth, and every tree whose fruit yields seed; to you it shall be for food."
>
> Genesis 1:28, 29 (NKJV)

These verses are filled with the perfect law of God's kingdom. They reveal his mindset. Here, he begins to describe life to the very first human beings, and it is a wonderful description of everything that they *can* do, *can* eat, *can* enjoy, *can* explore, and *can* experience. God's law was not given as a negative, restrictive burden to bear, but rather, as a gift to humankind.

I can imagine God coming in the cool of the day and walking with Adam through the garden, watching with pleasure as he discovered new animals to classify, flower-filled meadows, majestic waterfalls and perfect sunsets. The discoveries were endless. Everywhere they went, Adam found a broad array of fruits, vegetables, nuts, and herbs. Death and degeneration did not exist in his world, so the animals were herbivorous. Nothing preyed upon another. It was not even possible to crush

a flower or blade of grass to death. Man did not know the existence of harm or danger or fear or sadness. His energy was boundless, his life was rich and full, and his level of satisfaction is unfathomable by the modern mind. God had hidden treasures behind every bush and beyond every hill, just waiting to be found and enjoyed. Just about the time that Adam had decided on a favorite fruit, God would show him another variety that would leave him speechless with pleasure. Of course, the garden paradise was not the only work of perfection from God's artistic genius. This exquisite environment was solely designed to house and support God's creative masterpiece: The human being!

Modern man is said to use 3 to 6 percent of his mind's capacity. Albert Einstein may have used up to 10 percent according to some estimates. The intellect of God's first man would not have fallen short of its potential. Adam's mind functioned at the 100 percent level. His mind could instantly calculate anything within the scope of his vision—the number of blades of grass in the meadow, the leaves on any particular tree, and the astronomical movements in the night sky. The laws of physics would have been understood perfectly. His memory was instantaneous with no ability to forget. His grasp of math, biology, astronomy, chemistry, music, and the arts would have been incalculable by modern man. God had graced him with the ability to discern and decide all things with love and compassion, equity, and righteousness. His ability to manage the world was flawless in its efficiency and application.

The garden itself was perhaps quite large, possibly encompassing several hundred square miles. The Bible tells us of a river that flowed out of Eden and into the garden, parting into four riverheads, and the Bible also mentions the mineral wealth located in the various regions.

> And the Lord God commanded man saying, "Of every tree of the garden you may freely eat, but of the tree of knowledge of good and evil you shall not eat, for in the day that you eat of it you shall surely die."
>
> Genesis 2:16, 17 (NKJV)

God had given Adam his job description and spelled out the law of the kingdom clearly. He now, once again, reiterates all of the things that Adam *can* enjoy. It is at this time that God finally mentions the tree of knowledge of good and evil. He had spent a great deal of time showing and describing what man could have and now makes only one remark about the forbidden tree. God doesn't spend much time exhorting, warning, demonstrating, or illustrating just how important it is to stay away from the tree of knowledge of good and evil. He said it one time, and then proceeded to talk about Adam's need for a wife.

God, then causes a deep sleep to come over Adam and removes a "side" of him and places it within a separate human body. This new creation is a stunningly gorgeous woman, perfect in body and soul. Do you think Adam is concerned with the tree of knowledge of good and evil at this point? Are you kidding? He

has been totally amazed by all the wonders of creation, and now, an overwhelmingly beautiful woman stands before him. He can barely breathe!

What has just been described here is kingdom law as God originally intended! Adam's life is completely defined by this law, and his portion and allotment is well understood. The law of the kingdom of God can be summarized this way:

1. Mankind was to exercise authority over all creation.
2. Mankind was to be fruitful and multiply.
3. Mankind was to enjoy everything in his domain.
4. Mankind was to rest on the Sabbath day.
5. Mankind could not partake of the tree of knowledge of good and evil.

Five rules, and only one is an actual restriction. Is it beginning to get easier to pray for his kingdom to come? What would happen if our churches began to preach the law of the kingdom, instead of the typical dos and don'ts?

But it was in this kingdom paradise that mankind let down his guard. Some time before, Lucifer had been exiled to this very planet and now, by cunning and persistence, had managed to build some sort of rapport with the woman. His words captured her interest and convinced her to look at the forbidden tree. Desire was aroused in her heart, and she finally took some of its fruit and ate. Then she gave some to her husband, and he ate as well. Suddenly, they found themselves in a new world order with a different law system. God had

warned them that if they disobeyed him and ate of the tree of knowledge of good and evil, they would surely die. Some might argue that Adam and Eve did not actually die after eating the fruit. They lived out their lives, raised a family, and managed fairly well. Let's examine this more closely.

When God formed man from the soil of the earth, he breathed his divine life into the man, and the man became a living being. God created man to be a dwelling place for himself. The Holy Spirit had been breathed into Adam's being. Before God breathed into the man, he was perfectly formed but lifeless. Man began to live when Life Himself entered in. Now, after violating kingdom law, God, who is life, no longer had a place in the spirit of man. When life departs from a person's spirit or body, the void that remains is called death. So mankind did indeed die after he disobeyed because life moved out of his spirit, and death resulted. Things began to change rapidly. Fear, which had been absolutely unknown prior to this, now moved into their domain like a cold, dark mist. Animals grazing in the lush meadows began to raise their heads in alarm. An overwhelming sense of loneliness, emptiness, and dread swept over every living thing. Everything had changed. Welcome to the kingdom of Satan. God came on the scene and pronounced the punishment that they had earned. They were expelled from the garden lest they should eat from the tree of life. An animal gave its life to provide clothing, and death became the dominant force on planet Earth. Animals, once herbivorous, now began to prey upon other animals, blood began

to flow, thorns and thistles began to grow. Selfishness and rebellion tore through every particle of existence leaving their ugly fingerprints of chaos and dysfunction upon everything God had made. The law of the kingdom, which centered on freedom and enjoyment, was no longer the law of the earth. Lucifer had drawn man's attention to the one thing he could *not* have, and when the desire for what he could *not* have became strong, he reached out and took what he could *not* have and plunged the earth and everything on it into a new kingdom with a new law system, which is based upon everything you *cannot* have.

This new law system has at its core—fear, which God never intended man to experience. Today, the fear of danger prompts new restrictive laws of "safety." The fear of being offensive to others brings about "laws" of political correctness. Regulations rule every part of a human's life in the modern world. An ungodly system now claims the right to control our ability to travel, marry, build a house, discipline our children, and leave an inheritance. We are told that we live in a free country, but why then must we apply for a permit to do something that God gave us the freedom to do? The common concept of freedom is summed up in the phrase, *permission granted*. But even the permissible areas of our lives are subject to penalty. I believe that the American mentality is not much different than the nation of Israel's during their slavery years in Egypt. "Sure, we have to work hard while someone else takes the profit, but we have our families, we have our own homes, we have our sheep and cattle, and we can even spice our food with leaks, onions, and garlic. The governing authority will protect us from terrorists and provide security. Things aren't great, but they could be much worse."

Yes, Israel had cried out to God for deliverance, but when deliverance came, the true inward desires began to surface. It wasn't freedom that they really wanted; it was security. Here, the difference between a freeman and a slave comes to light: a freeman will sacrifice everything, including his own life to be truly free; a slave will concede freedom in order to be taken care of and have a sense of security.

Fear-Based "Christianity"

Six millennia have come and gone since that fateful moment in the garden of Eden. Six thousand years of living in a fear-based world. We cope with fear, rebellion, and death on a daily basis, which makes it very difficult to fathom a life that is much different. The Scriptures are the only point of reference that indicates to us that the life we know is substandard to God's original design. Since God never intended the human race to experience fear, he never equipped us with the ability to process it in our mind or emotions. Fear is an enemy to sound decision-making. The fear of getting into trouble causes certain people to follow every regulation, despite its origin, while others live with little regard to rules for fear of not experiencing life.

The religious leaders of Jesus's day had added so many regulations to everyday life that it was not even possible to live within their boundaries. Today, many good, well-meaning clergymen preach messages to their flock, with fear at its core. They are afraid that if people are not continually warned about the tree of knowledge of good and evil; they are not fulfilling their righteous duties and will be held accountable for everyone who strays. While it is certainly true that warnings must be issued from time to time, we must realize that if we are influenced by fear, we will preach restriction more than freedom in Christ. So fear-based Christianity points to sin over and over, describing it in detail lest we fail to understand what it is we are supposed to stay away from. We have been trying to communicate God's kingdom to people, using the philosophy of Satan's kingdom. Remember, God spent the bulk of his time pointing to what we *can* do, *can* enjoy, *can* experience, and only once did he mention the forbidden tree. It was Satan, not God, who drew Eve's attention to the one thing that was off limits. Many Christians have an incredible knowledge of sin. They can describe, in great detail, what their church is against and what they don't believe in and what kind of judgment awaits those who sin. But when asked to describe the freedom of the kingdom of God, many are at a total loss for words. Some church leaders, out of panic, might argue that if we spend more time preaching about all of the good things to enjoy, people may abuse this and exploit Christianity. After all, we must have safeguards against going too far. The truth of the matter is this, God gave gifts to the church that can easily be abused, and he doesn't seem worried about it. The Holy Spirit, in the Scriptures, spends far more time telling us how to use them to the benefit of everyone in the kingdom, than he does warning us about running wild with them. I certainly do not condone the misuse of the gifts in any way, but if the church is determined to err, then let it be on the side of freedom, not fear. God's kingdom is characterized by freedom. Fear is diabolical.

People will mishandle the spiritual gifts, and perhaps use them to manipulate others. There will be times when an unholy spirit of chaos and confusion tries to infiltrate. This is not a surprise. Forbidding the operation of the gifts of the Spirit certainly will not eliminate the potential for abuses within the church, and I am quite sure that God was well aware of all this when He bestowed those gifts. God should be far more concerned about this than we are, after all, it's *his* church. No, the real problem is that fearful people have decided to have a small, tidy, manageable Christianity. Some might say that it is better to withdraw from the charismatic gifts than to risk getting in the flesh. Admittedly, there is a certain amount of unholy flesh that can manifest, but it is far better to risk a little and step out in faith, than to sit back and resist the Holy Spirit. Those who resist the workings of the Holy Spirit are operating *completely* in the flesh while those who step out have a chance at getting it right, as they begin learning how to discern the difference between the mind of the flesh and the voice of the Spirit. The gift of salvation has been abused most, but no one is recommending that we give that up. Our eternal future rests on salvation through Christ, and we won't let go of that no matter who abuses it. And so it is with all of the gifts in Scripture. The health and wholeness of the church depends on them.

Outflow Of Grace

All the gifts come out of one grace.

> As each one has received a gift [charisma], minister it to one another, as good stewards of the manifold grace of God.
>
> 1Peter 4:10 (NKJV, brackets mine)

This verse clearly says that in order to be a good steward of God's grace, we must minister charisma to one another. This verse also indicates that the grace of God is manifold or multisided. A manifold has one inlet and many outlets, or many inlets and one outlet. The grace of God has one inlet because every good thing comes from God alone. But it has *many* outlets because there are many functions of grace. There is only one grace, but that grace has many facets. The Greek word *charisma* (*charis*, "grace"; and *ma*, "result or outflow") essentially means grace in action. If there is no outflow of grace, then there is no grace at all. It is not possible to have grace—*charis*—without having charisma, the result of grace. The grace of God is not static or motionless.

> For the wages of sin is death, but the gift [charisma] of God is eternal life in Christ Jesus our Lord.
>
> Romans 6:23 (NKJV, brackets mine)

This verse declares that the charismatic gift of eternal life has been given to us in Christ, once again proving that there is one multifaceted grace that contains everything. If the charismatic gifts passed away, as some teach, then salvation passed away also. But since God's grace is still flowing, then we are to drink from every outlet. No human being has ever had the right to preside over a piecemeal distribution of God's grace. If God doesn't recall his gifts because of mishandling, then neither should we. He simply gave us the most amazing gift ever given—without any fear. Let us put fear-based religion behind us forever and step into the joy of true freedom.

Bringing Balance

The Bible says in Hebrews 12 that our God is a consuming fire. I believe that the next major move of the Holy Spirit on this planet will bring us back to a knowledge of, and a respect for, the holiness of God.

In the late 1980s and early 1990s, I watched Christendom shift rapidly toward intimacy with God. There was a tremendous need to experience the Father's love and acceptance. Years before, the pendulum had swung toward legalistic rules and regulations and had finally reached its apex. People were sick and tired of "doing" Christianity and desperately craved a divine embrace. Emphasis on the Father's love, his unconditional acceptance, and intimacy with God swept through the church world, bringing welcome relief from the legalism of the previous era. The pendulum, however, was not swinging toward grace, but lawlessness. Now, twenty-five years later, we have a generation that seems to know nothing of God's holiness and his demand for purity in the lives of his people. They see themselves loved by God unconditionally, and therefore, somehow licensed to live as they wish. They boast "freedom in Christ" as they speak with irreverence and indiscretion. The "freedoms" that are practiced today, on a large scale are nothing more than fleshly indulgences, somehow justified by the philosophy that since law equals bondage, freedom from law *must* be grace. The opposite of law is, in fact, lawlessness, not grace. As I mentioned earlier in this chapter, the Greek word for law is *nomos*, which means "to parcel out by distribution or assignment, your portion, or your allotment." The opposite meaning would be derived by adding the negative particle *a* to the word *nomos*, creating the word *anomos*, which means "no portion and no allotment", and is translated *lawless*. The opposite of legalism is not grace, but lawlessness.

This concept will be explained fully in the next chapter, but for now, let it suffice to say that it is possible to fall off a horse on either side. In their hatred for legalism, and in their hurry to get away from it, many in Christendom have embraced lawlessness. But when it has reached the outer extreme, the church will be sickened by the sin, bondage, and depravity that this, so called freedom has produced, and will cry out for purity and holiness. This will be a good thing, initially, but the pendulum will swing all the way back to legalism in time.

Lawlessness

As I stated in the previous chapter, the Greek word for law is *nomos*, meaning "your portion, parcel, or allotment." Our English word *nominal* is a derivative and is commonly defined as "in name only." Law has, at its core, the idea of naming or defining what belongs to you and, thus, defines your life. Everything outside the boundaries of law does not belong to you. Freedom exists within the framework of this law system, and lawlessness exists without. The word for lawlessness in New Testament Greek is *anomos*, which is *nomos* (law) and the particle *a* (no or not) added as a prefix. Lawlessness is basically defined then as "*no* portion, *no* parcel, and *no* allotment." At its core, lawlessness is not actually "something" but rather the forfeiture of something.

How to Get Expelled From the Garden

When Satan came to Eve, he presented her with the thought that her life was somehow incomplete, that perhaps she was missing something, and that she actually had something to gain by taking his advice.

In reality, she had everything that pertains to life and godliness and lacked no good thing. But the only way to lure God's ultimate creation into a place of loss and emptiness was to sell them on the idea that there was a real, tangible "something" outside of the King's law. Lucifer himself had once stood at this very fork in the road. He had chosen to follow the exciting allurement of "more" that beckoned to his ego from just outside the boundary. The prospect of being more than the highest archangel was intoxicating. But it was not until his desire gave birth to action that his fingers closed around the nothingness that lawlessness really is. So he presented the same illusion that he had once fallen for, to the human family. The promise of more is a lie. Lawlessness, by practical definition, is a forfeiture of what one lawfully possesses. Lawlessness is the most expensive and least profitable purchase that can ever be made. It is giving up the solid freedom of life, the safety of home, and the substance of wealth; for nothing.

After his fall, Lucifer had become the proverbial "man without a country," a vagabond, the first one to be truly homeless, and now he was taking a vengeful jab at the King by convincing man to join him in his empty existence. Before long, Adam and Eve were experiencing the rewards of lawlessness: expulsion from the garden, separation from the life of God, degeneration of mind and body, and a terrible harshness emanating from the new overlord. Selfishness and rebellion form the liquid in Satan's bloodstream, and now that he was the spiritual daddy to every human being, it was inevitable that everyone would now be born with his spiritual

DNA, and the inescapable propensity to live out his ideals.

Lawlessness is the way of the satanic kingdom and the loss of inheritance, purpose, and identity is the commodity for sale, wrapped, of course, in the bright colorful promise of 'more'.

Knowledge or Wisdom?

Since that fateful day in Eden, man has been seeking knowledge on his way to enlightenment, with the promise that it all ends in immortality. In other words, *man believes that he can become like God!* Humankind has listened to the voice of the deceiver and chased knowledge right out of the garden. God, who epitomizes wisdom, knew that there were certain things that people, for their own preservation and well-being, should not know. But we ran away from wisdom in our quest for knowledge. The Bible teaches us that knowledge causes people to become puffed up in pride, but happy is the man who finds wisdom. Knowledge, apart from wisdom, will eventually lead to disaster. People with great intellectual knowledge often live self-centered, out-of-control lives, but those with wisdom tend to live more nobly, regardless of the facts they know or do not know. True wisdom walks with humility and draws us closer to God. Pride that accompanies mere knowledge compels us to live as if we *are* God.

Knowledge, and the search for it, has been glorified for ages, producing a culture that believes it is enough to know something, even if one does not practice it. But in reality, wisdom exists in the application of truth.

To merely know something is *never* enough; sometimes it is too much! The Bible says in Proverbs 4:7 (NKJV), "Wisdom is the principal thing; therefore get wisdom. And in all your getting, get understanding." If knowledge is the missile, then, wisdom is the missile's guidance system. Wisdom is to be sought after far more than knowledge alone. Wisdom is the ability to use knowledge correctly.

Christ Hates Lawlessness

> "You have loved righteousness and hated lawlessness; therefore God, Your God, has anointed You with the oil of gladness more than Your companions."
>
> Hebrews 1:9 (NKJV)

Why does God hate lawlessness? The answer to this question is found in understanding his true nature. God is absolutely selfless. This makes him the ultimate giver. He is love. The Bible does not say that God *has* love, but that he *is* love. God does not hate lawlessness because he is some egocentric, control freak who feels disrespected and threatened by someone with a different opinion. God hates lawlessness because he knows that you and I cannot afford to pay the price! His loving heart cannot stand to see us lose! He wants us to have something—a home, an identity, an inheritance in his kingdom! God's intense love for us actually compels him to have a hatred for that which would harm us.

Lawlessness is synonymous with forfeiture and loss; therefore, it is completely inconsistent with the kingdom of God.

> "Not everyone who says to Me, 'Lord, Lord,' shall enter the kingdom of heaven, but he who does the will of My Father in heaven. Many will say to Me in that day, 'Lord, Lord, have we not prophesied in Your name, cast out demons in Your name, and done many wonders in Your name?' And then I will declare to them, 'I never knew you: depart from Me, you who practice lawlessness!'"
>
> Matthew 7:21–23 (NKJV)

This passage does not, in any way, equate the casting out of demons or the working of miracles with lawlessness. The crucial message here is that the working of miracles does *not* equal justification. The ones standing before God, in this scenario, are defending their righteousness by listing their ministerial accomplishments. God does not say one word about the supernatural works, but cuts to the root of the matter: their personal practice of lawlessness. These people lived outside the framework of God's perfect law system, indulged in the nothingness of lawlessness, but then somehow expected to inherit the kingdom of heaven. God, in undeniable justice, measures out to them the reward of lawless living; the forfeiture of all that is real.

God loathes lawlessness because it keeps people from receiving and enjoying his goodness.

The Real Meaning of Sin

The New Testament Greek word for sin is *hamartia*, which literally means "to miss the mark." But we must look further because the revelation lies in the root word *hameros*, which is composed of the negative particle *a* (no or not) and *meros* (piece or portion), thus, meaning "no piece, no portion"—the same basic definition as lawlessness. Sin is lawlessness.

> Whoever commits sin also commits lawlessness, and sin is lawlessness.

> 1 John 3:4 (NKJV)

So why does God forbid sin? Is it because he just doesn't like it when people step over the line? No. When we sin, we lose our portion, and that is what God despises. The church has placed the emphasis on the wrong part. It has been understood and preached like this: "You have missed the mark!" The emphasis has been placed on the broken rule, but the heart of God does not grieve over a broken regulation. He grieves over the loss that his beloved child is about to experience. Jesus would probably preach it like this: "You have missed the mark *so as to lose your portion!*" This conveys the bottom line truth about sin: if people are warned about sin just because the rules need to be obeyed, the result usually resembles failure, and God is viewed as a cosmic kill joy who doesn't have a life and doesn't want us to have one either. But if God truly is love, then he is far more concerned with whether we win or lose than with the blind observance of law. Even our best attempts at warning a lost generation about sin and judgment, have oftentimes misrepresented the true nature of God.

Rules, Rules, Rules

Many people view God as one who loves his rules and who relishes the idea of crushing those who violate even the smallest one. God is not a lover of rules, but he does, however, love the benefits that his children enjoy when they keep them. God does not hate those who break the rules, but he simply despises that which harms his people.

The concept that stands behind the idea of rules, is training. There is a reason for every legitimate rule, and those being trained by them should accept them at face value until their understanding and wisdom increase enough to perceive the reasons behind the rules. The rule has then served its purpose.

> Therefore the law was our tutor to bring us to Christ, that we might be justified by faith. But after faith has come, we are no longer under a tutor.
>
> Galatians 3:24, 25 (NKJV)

The rules could even be removed from the life of a wise man without causing much change. Rules are for the novice, the inexperienced, and the childish who do not understand why things must be as they are. Here again, noble and common thinking part company. The wise and prudent see the rule for what it is—a servant to safeguard against harm until one can discern the right way for himself. A common thinker will undoubtedly view the rule as a master to be served, and when the feeling of restriction weighs upon him, he will seek to ignore and disobey the rule, not realizing that it is his thinking—not the rule—that is the real problem. Do you stop your car at an intersection because a sign commanded it? Or do you stop because there is cross-traffic and the possibility of a collision. The sign is there to serve us, not rule over us. The common thinker may feel choked and stifled by so many rules, but a wise man looks beyond the rule to find the reason for it, and having found it, sets it in his mind and enjoys the benefits of living by it. A truly wise person lives more by reason than by rules.

Transformed Thinking

Romans 12:2 (NKJV) says "...be transformed by the renewing of your mind." Notice first of all what this verse does *not* say. It does not say that you are transformed when you say the sinner's prayer. It does not say that you are transformed when you are baptized in the Holy Spirit. It says that you are transformed *when your mind is renewed.* A mind that thinks like unregenerate man has always thought, may not necessarily cause a forfeiture of salvation, but will certainly prevent him from walking in a high level of spiritual victory. A common thinking mind will not present itself useful in the hand of God for the advancement and growth of the kingdom. The dynamic power of God that is deposited in the heart cannot overrule the non-kingdom thought patterns of the mind.

> Now to Him Who is able to do exceedingly abundantly above all that we ask or think, according to the power that works in us.
>
> Ephesians 3:20 (NKJV)

Let me offer a paraphrase of this verse for your consideration.

> The limitless power of God is available to perform miracles beyond our wildest imagination, but the amount of power that *we allow* to operate in our lives, will be our total experience.

So what is the limiting factor in the lives of born again Christians? The non-kingdom paradigm that usurps authority over the spirit of God within! The Bible tells us in 2 Corinthians 10:5 to cast down the arguments of the mind. The word translated *arguments*, is the Greek word *logismos*, from which our English word *logic* is derived. It means "mindset or paradigm," not just casual or single thoughts. This verse is referring to the reasoning and rationale of a person. We are instructed here to cast down, or dethrone our old thought patterns, abandon our old philosophy, determine that our logic system is faulty, and allow it to be removed. When God is free to install a kingdom mindset within us, we are truly transformed!

An Internal Law

> But this is the covenant that I will make with the house of Israel after those days, says the Lord: I will put My law in their minds, and write it on their hearts; and I will be their God, and they shall be My people.
>
> Jeremiah 31:33 (NKJV)

The law of the kingdom of God is designed to be an internal law. The Bible says that grace does not do away with the law, but rather fulfills it. Grace causes the law of God to move inside of a person. So what law system are we referring to? Certainly not the law of restriction! God would never put within his people the law system that has been in operation *since* the fall of man. He will place within us the law system that governed the earth *before* the fall, the perfect law of freedom. Not the Ten Commandments. Not the levitical law. Not manmade rules for your "safety". His law is the law of love.

In one of Jesus's parables, a king is about to leave on a long journey, and so he gives three of his servants some money and tells them to do business until he returns. To the first one he gives five talents; to another, he gives two; and to the last servant, he gives one talent. While the king is gone, the servants with five talents and two talents invest wisely and double their master's money. The third servant finds a safe place, digs a hole, and buries the talent. When the king finally returns, he calls his servants and asks them to give an account to him. The first two are excited to tell their master about their success. The king said to each of them, "Well done, good and faithful servant, you have been faithful over a few things, I will make you ruler over many things, enter into the joy of your Lord!" The last servant, to whom one talent had been given, brought it to the king, hoping that his master would be pleased enough that he had not lost it. The king took it from him, judged him to be wicked, and threw him out of the kingdom.

The law of God's kingdom is an internal law, not something we are compelled to do by outside forces. The servant with one talent had lawlessness in his heart. As soon as the accountability factor was gone, he simply put kingdom living on hold; buried his calling, purpose and responsibility; and lived for himself. He figured that the king would be satisfied that the money wasn't lost, but the king could have stored his money against loss in a dusty vault. The king is an investor, so he was angry at the man's indifference. The servant did not really care whether the kingdom prospered or not, and it was that attitude that disqualified him from living there.

The successful servants conducted their lives as though their king was still present. The noble purpose of the kingdom had become more than an external demand. It had become part of their own hearts' desire. When the external forces are removed, it will become apparent if the law of the kingdom is within the heart.

Law, Lawlessness, and Grace

For several millennia, people groups have embraced a particular law system only to watch it become a system of legalistic enslavement. There is usually some sort of rebellion, and then, the answer that they thought was so perfect becomes as destructive as the first. This cycle has operated within the church as well. On one end of the pendulum's arc, we have law in all of its restriction and judgment. When good people are tired of being strangled by legalism, they cry out for grace and freedom in Christ, and the pendulum swings the other way. But as we stated earlier, grace is not the opposite of law. Lawlessness is the opposite of law. Law on one side, no law on the other. When people have had their fill of pharisaical rules and regulations, they often swing toward lawlessness and begin to indulge in all of the things that the law forbids and succeed only in losing the freedom and blessing that they so desperately craved. Then after a while, some begin to take an honest look at the horrible results that their "freedom" produced, and a cry for holiness, righteousness, and the fear of the Lord is heard throughout the land, and the pendulum begins its journey back again.

The pendulum described here is as ungodly as its creator. Satan designed it, and in all reality does not care where you are in its cycle. His diabolical law of restriction stands on one side, and his ability to steal your allotment, piece, and portion stands on the other. But the moment that we rise up with renewed minds and embrace the law of the kingdom, we step onto the unshakeable foundation of God's grace. No longer tossed to and fro on the waves of Satan's lies, we stand firm on the immoveable Rock of our salvation. Get off the pendulum! God doesn't want his people to rise and fall with the tide! His word to us is steadfast and sure; it doesn't change.

Contrary to what some may believe, grace is not God's attitude toward our lawlessness, neither is it forgiveness. Grace is empowerment. The Bible tells us that from Adam until Moses, there was no official written law, and so consequently, there could be no penalty for law breaking. "For until the law sin was in the world, but sin is not imputed when there is no law" (Romans 5:13, NKJV). During this particular time in history, people lived without condemnation even though they were falling far short of the righteousness of God. After many years, the law was given and God spelled out precisely what was expected of mankind. The bar of expectation was incredibly high, and most people quickly realized that it was not humanly possible to measure up.

Years later, Jesus Christ came and fulfilled the requirements of the law with ease and demonstrated what a grace-empowered life looks like. Then, through his death and resurrection, the gift of grace was offered to mankind so that everyone who is connected to Christ can also clear the bar and please God. Grace is the power to exceed the law. When we live a grace-empowered life, the law can be removed without any effect. This is why Jesus said, "Do not think that I came to destroy the Law or the prophets. I did not come to destroy but to fulfill" (Matthew 5:17, NKJV). The law can *only* be removed if a person is exceeding its requirements by the grace of God. Grace is not God's acceptance of a life that consistently falls short of kingdom righteousness. Many people have the mistaken idea that God somehow requires less in the New Testament than he did in the Old Testament. This is not true. He still loves what he loves and hates what he hates; the bar is still at the same level. God's grace enables us to consistently surpass the law's requirements, which makes it possible to remove the law because it is no longer needed. Grace has taken over and accomplished what the law could never do. It enabled us to hit the mark and be righteous and acceptable to God.

Freedom in Christ

The concept of freedom is very misunderstood by the unrenewed mind. Many times, I have heard a person say with indignation, "It's my life, I can do whatever I want." These people believe that freedom is the ability to *do* anything that one pleases. But true freedom is the state of being liberated *from* something. A person who takes their freedom and uses it to injure someone else has just waived their right to be free. In reality, no one is free to do as they please, for this is lawlessness. No one is free to do the wrong thing; we are only free to do the right thing. Ironically enough, unbridled liberty will enslave you. Freedom, as it is understood by pendulum swingers, is nothing more than selfish indulgence thumbing its nose at the law of restriction. Freedom in Christ is found in exploring the riches of God's grace, tasting of the hidden manna, drinking in the purity of the Spirit, and not allowing anyone to sell you on the idea that you are missing out because you refrain from the tree of knowledge of good and evil. I am not *free to indulge* my natural desires. I am *free from* the captivity that results from indulgence.

The Hebrew word for freedom is *derowr*, from a root word meaning "to move rapidly, freedom," hence spontaneity of outflow or movement. The Greek word for liberty, *eleutheros*, means "free born, exempt from legal obligation." The verb form, *eleuthomai* means "to come or go." These words speak of the ability to move or travel in an unrestricted manner. If uninjurious movement or travel is inhibited or regulated, then freedom—by definition—does not exist. John 8:36 (NKJV) says, "Therefore if the Son makes you free, you shall be free indeed."

True freedom exists only in Christ Jesus.

The Lawless One

A lawless person, by definition, is one who has forfeited their place, their portion, and their allotment. The Bible identifies the Antichrist as the man of lawlessness or the lawless one. We know that he will embody the nature and purpose of Satan and will be exalted to power by the kingdom of darkness. The Antichrist will ultimately have the same reward as Lucifer himself—nothing. Because Satan traffics in lawlessness, he doesn't have a tangible product to sell or a real service to offer. He has nothing. The darkness that is in him is simply the void where light once lived. Coldness and hatred exist in him because the warmth of God's love is no longer welcome. Satan epitomizes void. He is empty, his kingdom is empty, and his followers are also empty. He forfeited everything and grasped hold of nothing. The substance and reward of pride and selfishness is, in fact, nothing.

His salesmanship has been superb, however, because he acts as though he has a wonderful "something" to offer, and since Eve gave up everything in order to participate in nothingness, her offspring have had the natural inclination to do the same. Deception is used to gain control of people, and the deception is carefully maintained in order to keep them. Satan now directs their attention away from their emptiness of heart and constantly reaffirms their freedom in self-centered living.

He forfeited his place, lost his portion and discarded his inheritance by grasping for the *forbidden* thing, and realized all too late that he was the possessor of all emptiness and nothingness. Those who believe his lies and take part in his kingdom will receive the same reward. Nothing.

One of the names by which Satan is called is Apollyon. This Greek name means "destroyer." The root word *appolumi* from which Apollyon is derived, means "to be lost." Once again, the great Lost One rises up to deceive.

He is also known as the ruler of darkness. As we all know, darkness is not a substance, but the *absence* of a substance. His kingdom consists of the absence of anything real.

Illegitimate Rules

I have stated that there must be just cause for a rule or law, but a quick look at our society will reveal the fact that not all rules have a good reason behind them. If there is not a legitimate reason for the rule, then, it is the responsibility of the wise and prudent to render it null and void. A law without a beneficial and legitimate reason behind it is truly oppressive. When laws benefit one social group and place burden upon another, this is oppression. When you find yourself serving rules, which are counterproductive or unjust, you are living under oppression. Tyrants, all through history, have preyed upon the common thinking person because it is possible to incrementally take their liberty from them by dangling more and more benefits and slowly adding more regulations. They will always cry and complain about their decreasing freedom, but they will follow the rules because they serve rules, not reason. It then becomes the responsibility of the wise, by default, to contest and overthrow the unjust laws and unreasonable rules. It is stated in the Unanimous Declaration (July 4, 1776): "It is the right of the people to alter or abolish…it is their right; it is their duty, to throw off such government." The Unanimous Declaration also states, "and accordingly all experience hath shewn, that mankind are more disposed to suffer, while evils are sufferable, than to right themselves by abolishing the forms to which they are accustomed." It seems that common thinkers always outnumber the wise.

See + Contemplate = Desire

> So when the woman *saw* that the tree was good
> for food, that it was *pleasant to the eyes*, and a
> tree *desirable* to make one wise, she took of its
> fruit and ate. She also gave to her husband with
> her, and he ate.
>
> Genesis 3:6 (NKJV, emphasis mine)

The turning point of the human race is found in this verse. One of the most powerful lessons in human nature is found there as well: The human being is drawn to that which he sees. Unfortunately, very few humans, comparatively speaking, ever realize how the desires lodged within them even got started. Most people just accept every desire that rises up within the mental and emotional realm as an inseparable part of their personality. The common thinking person will simply accept their own feelings and desires, and seek to satisfy them, usually at an unreasonable cost while the noble-minded will actually challenge their own emotions so as not to be governed by them.

"Desire is aroused by what we see." Let us now carefully examine this concept.

From the account of Eve's temptation in Genesis 3:6, we can see that the spark of desire ignited when her attention was drawn to the forbidden tree. Now, I realize that she was listening to a very slick sales pitch, but her desire began to rise when she *looked* at this tree with a new interest. The old saying "you can look but you can't touch," simply doesn't work. The desire to touch comes from the act of looking! As we begin to focus our attention on something, our brain becomes increasingly filled with wishful thinking, and soon desire is produced within us, and there is little else on our mind. I call this concept "See + Contemplate = Desire."

The marketing industry uses this formula all the time. If they can keep the image of something in front of your eyes, they have a better chance of selling it to you.

Conversely, the concept can be used to produce indifference toward that which is normally abhorrent. The very same enemy that used this tactic on Eve is still relying on it to accomplish his evil agenda today.

Many years ago, people were outraged at the idea of legalized abortion and same-sex marriage in this country. But these sins have been "advertised" so often that now even within the church world, there is mild-mannered tolerance, if not outright acceptance of them. The television and movie industry has progressively shown more violence, sex, and blatant anti-Christian sentiment over the past several decades, but the American populace has not put a stop to it because the more it is in front of our eyes, the more accustomed to it we have become.

How did Jesus Christ live a pure life when he walked among humanity? Was it because he was God? The answer is no! Christ allowed the limitations of humanity to be placed upon him in order to be a legitimate example for us. But how did he do it? The key is found in Acts 2:25 (NKJV), "For David says concerning Him: 'I foresaw the Lord always before my face, for He is at my right hand, that I may not be shaken.'"

Jesus, the Messiah, practiced the principle that we are examining here: You will desire those things that are before your face. Christ, as a man, kept the image of God before his eyes, so his desire was always toward the Lord. Scripture also says in Hebrews 12:2 (NKJV), "Looking unto Jesus, the author and finisher of our faith, Who for the joy that was set before Him, endured the cross, despising the shame."

Once again, we see our Lord looking past the cross and focusing on the joy that it would produce. The first part of the verse is an admonishment for us to follow Christ's example. The word *looking*, in this verse, comes from the Greek word *aphorao*, which signifies undivided attention, the refusal to look at certain things in order to steadfastly fix one's eyes upon something else. Just as Jesus did, we are to look away from our present difficulties and temptations and fix our gaze upon the prize at the end of the race.

The lesson becomes clear: the first Adam lost everything in the garden of Eden because he considered the wrong thing while the Second Adam won his battle in the garden of Gethsemane by looking at the divine plan of God instead of his own will.

Consider also Abraham who is known as the father of our faith. What can we learn from a man, who for the first twenty-four years of his relationship with God, only knew him in a basic sense? He did not have a Bible to read. He couldn't attend church on the Lord's Day and hear a rousing sermon on the integrity of God's Word. So what kept him strong in faith? Romans 4:19–21 (NKJV, emphasis mine) contains the simple strategy of this great patriarch.

> And not being weak in faith, he *did not consider* his own body, already dead (since he was about one hundred years old) and the deadness of Sarah's womb. He did not waver at the promise of God through unbelief, but was strengthened in faith, giving glory to God and being fully convinced that what he had promised, he was also able to perform.

Abraham simply *would not consider* the physical obstacles that stood in opposition to the promise of God. The Bible speaks of the heroes of faith in the book of Hebrews.

> These all died in faith, not having received the promises, but having *seen* them afar off were *assured of them, embraced them and confessed* that they were strangers and pilgrims on the earth. For those who say such things declare plainly that they seek a homeland. And truly if they had *called to mind* that country from which they had come out, they would have had opportunity to return. But now they *desire* a better, that is, a heavenly country.
>
> Hebrews 11:13–16a (NKJV, emphasis mine)

Those who succeed are always looking toward success. Those who look back at the bondage they were rescued from will develop a strong desire to return. We must be careful what we see! Vision comes first, then faith, and then movement toward that which is visualized. This simple law of humanity works whether it is aimed at the right things or the wrong things.

Modern Christians, in regard to problems in their life, have been asking the wrong question "How much faith is enough faith?" When the crucial question is, and always has been, "How much unbelief is *too much*?" The Bible tells us in Romans 12:3 that God has given to each one of us a measure of faith. We are also told in Matthew 17:20 and in Luke 17:6 that faith as a mustard seed is enough to move mountains. It is clear from these verses that God has already placed faith in our hearts, and even if it is comparable to a tiny mustard seed, it is still enough to relocate a mountain into the ocean! So why aren't more mountains being removed? The answer is very simple. It is because of unbelief.

Unbelief naturally results from looking at and considering the problem. Faith, of course, comes from looking *away from* the problem, and fixing our gaze upon the word of God and considering nothing else!

> And Peter answered Him and said, "Lord, if it is
> You, command me to come to You on the water."
> So He said, "Come." And when Peter had come
> down out of the boat, he walked on the water to
> go to Jesus. But *when he saw* that the wind was
> boisterous, he was afraid: and beginning to sink
> he cried out, saying, "Lord, save me!"
>
> Matthew 14:28–30 (NKJV, emphasis mine)

When was fear generated in Peter's heart? *When he saw* that the wind was boisterous. Faith is free to operate when we *do not look at the obstacle*, but look at the supernatural word of God. The lesson here is that *we will never receive a supernatural answer, by looking at a natural problem.*

Let me create a modern scenario to illustrate this point.

A young wife detects a lump in her breast, so she schedules an examination. The doctor persuades her to undergo a biopsy, and the test comes back positive. The growth is malignant. It is at this point that she makes her largest tactical error. She begins to research the problem! She spends hours searching the internet for information about her cancer. She learns to pronounce the medical name for it, she finds out statistically how many women have this type of cancer and how aggressive it is, and she investigates treatment options. She spends a great deal of time preparing mentally, emotionally, and financially for this "fight," and is very faithful to her scheduled checkups to see how fast the tumor is growing.

By this time, there is an emotional identification process happening. It now has a "place" in her life, and she begins to wonder, "Do I have enough faith to receive healing?" The answer is yes, she does have enough faith. God measured out "enough faith" to her. The problem is that her mustard seed sized faith is buried under an avalanche of unbelief! She fueled her unbelief by researching the problem until it loomed larger in her situation than God's covenant word! *Abraham did exactly the opposite!* He refused to consider anything but God's word to him. Abraham would not allow anyone to talk to him about the physical odds, and he would not allow his own thoughts to "face the facts" about the situation. He just simply *would not* smother his faith with a negative report.

Then comes the inevitable argument, "Well, I think we should know all about the problem, so we can pray specifically against it." First of all, scripture does not teach us to pray *against* things. The idea of "praying against" something is manmade.

Secondly, as we pray *for* the answer, we can be very specific. The Bible says in James 5:15 that the "prayer of *faith* will save the sick"; however, many times it is not a prayer of faith that is offered, but a detailed description of the problem!

Thirdly, this line of reasoning is first encountered in Genesis chapter 3, where Satan suggested to Eve that she was somehow incomplete unless she *knew* evil as well as good. This incident set precedence in the fallen world and chasing after "knowledge" instantly became the ultimate priority. *The concept of knowing all about the problem originated in the mind of Satan!* And no matter how many times I read the scriptural account, Eve always loses because of it!

I am in no way advocating ignorance in a general sense, but your enemy knows that if he can get you to focus on the problem, you will forfeit the blessed life every time. Satan knew that this temptation would be effective because he himself had once fallen for it. When he took his eyes off God and began to admire his own beauty, he became intoxicated by foolish pride until he could no longer see the reality around him. He was blinded to the fact that God is *infinite*, and he is *finite*. The fact that it is absolutely impossible for a finite being to overthrow the infinite being apparently escaped him.

> He said in his heart, "I will be *like* the Most High."
>
> Isaiah 14:14 (NKJV, emphasis mine)

Satan reached out for more and lost what he had! So, he convinced Eve that she could "be *like* God" (Genesis 3:5, NKJV), and sure enough, she lost her place in God's kingdom. The devil has been peddling the idea of "enlightenment" to mankind ever since, knowing that it appeals to us to be like God, but never telling us that we forfeit everything by chasing after it! This satanic paradigm has threaded its way into the universal fabric of human thought, even theological thought, and has set us up for failure. The young woman who considers and contemplates her cancer will most likely forfeit the healing that has been hers in Christ for two thousand years, not because she doesn't have enough faith, but because she has fallen victim to the oldest trick in the book: what you see and think about will overcome you!

The man who focuses on his struggle with pornography will always be overpowered by it. The person who rehearses an offense over and over in their mind will have great difficulty forgiving the wrongdoer. If we would consistently set our mind on the right things, much of our battle would simply go away. People struggle with things that are fueled by their own thoughts, and then blame it on the devil. The enemy isn't even around most of the time. Their life is on "autopilot," flying on a crash course, so the enemy just checks on them from time to time to make sure that they haven't figured it out.

What you meditate on will certainly control you.

I heard Andrew Wommack once said, "You cannot be tempted with something you will not think about." This empowering truth, in all of its simplicity, is staggering! Overcoming sin is not difficult when we understand how the desire for it is fueled. If we consider what God's word says, we will receive what God's word says. If we meditate on the problem, then we will receive everything that the problem has to offer. You will, undoubtedly, be accused of living in denial if you don't research the problem, but that is simply not true. We *do* acknowledge the existence of the problem, then immediately turn our attention to the word of God so that we can strengthen our faith, eliminate doubt and fear, and firmly grasp our victory. We do not deny the *existence* of a problem; however, we are denying it the *right to continue* in our lives.

Let us consider a few more examples in the Scriptures.

During the battle of Jericho, a man named Achan took some of the forbidden treasure and brought severe judgment upon himself, his family, and his entire nation. In Joshua 7:21, he describes how he fell into disobedience:

> When I *saw* among the spoils a beautiful
> Babylonian garment, two hundred shekels
> of silver, and a wedge of gold weighing fifty
> shekels, I coveted them and took them. And
> there they are, hidden in the earth in the midst
> of my tent, with the silver under it.

Achan was essentially saying, "I saw it, I thought about it, I desired it and then I took it." Sometimes the entire process takes only a moment. King David, in 2 Samuel 11:2, *saw* a beautiful woman named Bathsheba bathing. He obviously did not turn his thoughts away from her, because in verse 3, he sent someone to find out more about her. The more he indulged his mind with images of this beautiful naked woman, the more desire was awakened within him. When David found out that she was the wife of Uriah the Hittite, one of his original four hundred men and a longtime friend, he took her anyway. His desire had reached a fever pitch and his sense of reasoning was buried beneath an avalanche of emotion.

Even after accidentally seeing Bathsheba bathing, David was innocent because one cannot always control what falls in front of one's eyes. But from that point on it was within his power to decide. We, like David, will always have the choice to turn our attention away from temptation, causing desire to fade away, or indulge our mind at the pleading of our emotions and forfeit another victory.

Unintentional Enablers

The whole of Scriptures can be categorized into two basic themes:

1. God's dealings with mankind in love and power
2. Man's struggle to obey and serve God

All good-willed church leaders will point toward one or the other. They will either point toward all the trees in the garden that have been freely given, or they will enable, perhaps unintentionally, the kingdom of darkness as they draw attention to that which is forbidden. Preachers and teachers that instruct their people about God's love and power toward mankind will probably have a flock that is living and operating with more spiritual success than those who continually talk about man's struggle to serve God. Those who focus on the latter will "help" their congregations stay in a struggling mode. Many well-meaning church leaders have perpetuated a sense of inadequacy, faithlessness, and disobedience in the lives of their parishioners by constantly pointing to it. Some have preached on it so much that their people know little else.

But the all important question to ask is this: how can we keep from inadvertently promoting sin in our zeal to promote righteousness? The answer is simple. We must renew our minds. Just because you have accepted Christ as Lord and Savior and received a new heart filled with the kingdom of God does not mean that your mind is automatically aligned with kingdom principles. Your spirit was reborn, but your mind must be retrained!

As Adam and Eve stood with the forbidden fruit still between their teeth, their citizenship was transferred to the kingdom of Satan, and their transformation into *his* image was begun. As I stated earlier in this book, the law of this new kingdom always points toward what you should not do, thus ensuring that people will always do those very things. Why? Because desire is aroused by what we see and think about.

Many good Christian leaders have stood before their congregations with the kingdom of God in their hearts and the methods of the kingdom of darkness still firmly planted in their minds. They point over and over to the sins and snares of evil, they warn their beloved people again and again, and they wonder why their congregants seem to do the very things that they're told not to do. Here is the bottom line: you cannot advance the kingdom of God with the tactics of the enemy. You cannot motivate your people to live with a supernatural mindset by reminding them of their natural inclinations. You cannot elevate their devotion to God by preaching at their disobedience. The Apostle Paul said in Romans 7:8, "But sin, taking opportunity by the commandment, produced in me all manner of evil desire. For apart from the law sin was dead." Paul acknowledges here that the law of restriction, despite its noble intent, is producing desire for the very sin it is warning us against. That is why God will never write *this* law in our hearts. It would be counterproductive.

Good Shepherds

We are told in Psalm 23 that the shepherd leads his sheep to green pastures, beside still waters, and in the paths of righteousness. A good shepherd does not continually warn his sheep of the dangers of thorns and thistles, cliffs, and wolves. The gospel message is the good news of the kingdom, but it is often given with an emphasis on all of the manmade warnings, cautions, and disclaimers. God would much rather have us shepherd his church out of a love for people than a fear of accountability. So let us simply present the gospel the way the King would do it—freedom focused, not fear based. Yes, the freedom of God can be misused and exploited, but that doesn't seem to worry the King, so don't let it worry you. He has a perfect record-keeping system and will measure out flawless judgment to the abusers at the right time. He didn't call us into spiritual law enforcement. Let's just lead people to green pastures and still waters, making sure they are fed and protected. This is the act of shepherding.

Call It Like You See It

We have all heard it said, "I just call it like I see it," and we all, to one degree or another, live by this code. The challenge for Christ's followers is that we must "see" things differently than we used to. It is necessary that we see the way our King sees.

As the Supreme Creator, he constantly sees things the way they *should* be, not merely the way they *are*. When God looked at the earth as described in Genesis 1:2, he was well aware of its dark, shapeless, lifeless condition, but he *saw* the exquisite design that he intended to create and infused his awesome power into that vision. He did not look at the earth and say, "Wow, it's dark out there!" If he had, his creative word would have been released to hold the world in darkness. Romans 4:17 lets us know that God calls those things which do not exist, as though they did. He spoke light *before* there was light. That is creativity! God promised Abram and Sarai a son and, then, changed Abram's name to Abraham (father of a multitude) long before he had children. God called him a father *before* he was a father.

I remember reading the story of Gideon in the book of Judges. During this particular time in Israel's history, the Midianites, a vicious group of people, were oppressing and terrorizing them. The Midianites would wait until the Israeli farmers had raised their crops and harvested them, and then would swoop down, raid, plunder, and destroy, leaving the people of Israel impoverished and starving. But a certain young Israelite had a cunning idea: why not take his wheat and thresh it in the winepress? The Midianites would be looking for him at the threshing floor, not the winepress! One day, while he is threshing his wheat in the winepress, hiding from the enemy, the angel of the Lord appears to him and says, "The Lord is with you, you mighty man of valor!"

I remember chuckling to myself at this "mighty man of valor" hiding in the winepress. It was then that the voice of the Lord hit me with a question. "Do you think I was being sarcastic?"

I knew that God has no disrespectful qualities, and so I very meekly answered, "No, Sir." The Lord spoke again, "I was not being sarcastic. I needed a mighty man of valor, so I was *creating one*." Why hadn't I seen that before? God *always* speaks the end result from the beginning! With a new humility and admiration for God, I realized that I had been *seeing* Gideon as a scared, weak, little wimp, which is why God's words to him seemed out of place. God, on the other hand, was *seeing* the mighty man of valor that was needed to deliver Israel and was simply infusing his creative word into *that* image.

Another example is found in the history of Israel. From the beginning of their journey through the wilderness, the Israelites had been grumbling, complaining, and threatening mutiny whenever they encountered a hardship. They would accuse Moses and God of bringing them out into the desert to die. So as the people neared the southern border of Canaan, the Lord told Moses to send spies into the land to see if it was all that had been promised. Of course, God knew that the land was wonderful, but he wanted his people to be encouraged by the news. Upon their return, the twelve spies began to report. One after another began to say that the land was indeed all that God had promised, but that it could not be conquered. The inhabitants of the land were too strong.

Two of the spies were appalled at the report of the majority and quickly spoke up and declared that Israel was well able to take possession of the land. But the ten spies spoke vehemently.

> "We are not able to go up against the people, for they are stronger than we." And they gave the children of Israel a bad report of the land which they had spied out saying, "The land through which we have gone as spies is a land that devours its inhabitants and all the people whom we saw in it are men of great stature. There we saw the giants (the descendants of Anak came from the giants); and *we were like grasshoppers in our own sight*, and so we were in their sight." So all the congregation lifted up their voices and cried, and the people wept that night.
>
> Numbers 13:31–33 (NKJV, emphasis mine)

God became extremely angry and judged the men who had brought the evil report and they died by a plague. Then, God passed sentence upon the people because that had believed the evil report and taken sides against his word.

> Say to them, "As I live," says the Lord, "Just as you have spoken in My hearing, so I will do to you: The carcasses of you who have complained against me shall fall in this wilderness."
>
> Numbers 14:28 (NKJV)

The people had been *seeing* their own demise in the desert, they had been *calling it* with their mouth, and now God says essentially, "What you have said is what you are going to get."

The truth of the matter is this: not even God Almighty can keep you from receiving those things that you *see and speak*!

So the question is, "What do you see?" If we "call it like it is," it will probably stay that way. But if we can see what our King sees, think the way our King thinks, and speak his words into that image, we will recreate his kingdom in our world.

Think on These Things

> This book of the law shall not depart from your mouth, but you shall meditate in it day and night, that you may observe to do according to all that is written in it. For then you will make your way prosperous, and then you will have good success.
>
> Joshua 1:8 (NKJV)

These words from the mouth of God himself show us the "recipe" for success. If we are to truly prosper in everything we do, we must live in complete alignment with God's kingdom. In order to maintain proper alignment, we must have it on our mind, this is why God instructs us to meditate on his words day and night. If we constantly think about the word of God, then, we are *not* worrying, entertaining temptation or thinking about selfish indulgence. People who consistently occupy their mind with God's word will be sensitive to the voice of the Spirit as he directs their steps.

> You will keep him in perfect peace, whose mind is stayed on You, because he trusts in You.
>
> Isaiah 26:3 (NKJV)

The Lord had been speaking this verse to me several times a day for a few weeks. Being the astute man that I am, I told myself that when I had more time, I was going to sit down and figure out what he was trying to communicate to me. About six months later, amid inner turmoil and emotional pain, I heard him say it one more time. I remember asking him what he was trying to get across to me. The voice of the Spirit instantly, and rather firmly responded, "I couldn't keep you in perfect peace because you wouldn't keep your mind stayed on me!" Well, that made perfect sense! I really don't know how I could have missed it. That is exactly what the verse is trying to communicate to us.

At first, I wasn't exactly sure what to meditate on, but after a while, I realized that I needed to think through a story or scenario in the Scriptures, not just repeat a verse over and over. I began, in my imagination, to walk with Jesus from the last supper to his ascension into heaven. I visualized every detail. Sometimes, I would stop what I was doing and open my Bible to see if I was remembering correctly. Before long, the Holy Spirit began to take me to other passages that revealed more about Christ's redemptive work. Within a few days, I was completely immersed in a Bible study that completely changed my life.

Sometime later, I suddenly realized that all of the emotional anguish was gone; *I was walking in perfect peace*. I could remember all the things that had hurt me, but now, there was no pain. I was *seeing* the word, *contemplating* the word, and the blessings of God had overwhelmed me. Philippians 4:7 is absolutely true; the peace of God transcends all logical reasoning.

God had given me perfect peace, but that was not the ultimate gain. As I meditated on the kingdom of God, he began to unveil my mind to many things in scripture and pour his revelation knowledge into me until, at times, I was certain I couldn't contain any more. I felt as though I had walked into an unknown realm through a door called meditation.

The word *meditate* comes from the Hebrew word *hagah*, meaning "to reflect, to moan, to mutter, to ponder, to make a quiet sound such as sighing, to meditate or contemplate something as one repeats the words." Hagah represents something quite unlike the English *meditation*, which may be a mental exercise only. (Word Wealth at Psalm 1:2, Spirit Filled Life Bible) Meditating, as God instructs, is not *emptying* the mind, humming, or repeating a mantra, it is allowing your mind to be *filled* with the riches of God's wisdom.

The Bible says in Philippians 4:8, "Finally, brethren, whatever things are true, whatever things are noble, whatever things are just, whatever things are pure, whatever things are lovely, whatever things are of good report, if there is any virtue and if there is anything praiseworthy—meditate on these things."

If we used this verse as the "measuring stick" for our thought life, all of the worry, unbelief, and offense would have little or no place in our minds, and thus, no control in our lives.

Serving God is not hard, if that is what you're thinking about. Life gets very tough when we think about the wrong things while trying to do the right things.

What you and I consistently think about, is what governs our lives.

Do What Kings Do

People are different.

It is true that God created all men equal in value, but that is where equality ends. There are some people who rise above mediocrity and do great things while others are content to aim at the minimum requirement and follow the road well traveled. I do not believe that some people are highborn, while others are of low birth. I deplore the concept of social caste. No one is born better than anyone else; however, there are observable differences in the ways that people choose to live. Since the beginning of time, there have been good people who seemed to see a world of endless possibilities. These people, regardless of rank or social standing, have gone against the odds, challenged conventional thought, and, in many cases, reshaped the history of the world. We shall refer to them as kings. There are others who are content to cope with whatever comes their way. They seem to view the world as they are instructed. These people, many of sterling character, never dare to set precedence. This is the most common way to live.

I am convinced that it is neither pedigree nor circumstance that causes a person to exist or to excel, but rather, their way of thinking. In this chapter, we will examine the differences between commoners and kings.

Who Am I?

First, we must ask the all-important question: who am I in the kingdom of God? It is imperative that we understand and embrace our identity in Christ Jesus. Many Christians simply do not know what the Bible has to say about them and their role in the kingdom. What happens to a person when they receive Christ as Savior? Are they merely forgiven? Is there more to it than that?

Scripture points out in Colossians 1:12, 13 that we have been qualified by God to partake of the inheritance of the saints and that he has delivered us from the power of darkness and conveyed us into the kingdom of his son. Ephesians 2:5, 6 clearly indicates that those who live in the kingdom of Satan (every human being is born into it) are in a state of spiritual death. But God, by his grace, made a way for us to become spiritually alive. It is by accepting Jesus Christ's work of redemption. This does not mean that we are only forgiven, but it also involves a new birth, a new spiritual father, a new spiritual DNA. It involves a transfer of citizenship from one kingdom to the other, a new law system, a new identity, a new king, a new purpose, a new position of authority, and a new destiny! Ephesians 2:19 says that we are members of the household of God! This is catastrophic change! This is where human language becomes very inadequate. Who can really grasp the fullness of redemption?

In spite of all this, many Christians do not live much differently after salvation than they did before. Why? Romans 12:2 supplies the answer. "And do not be conformed to this world, but be transformed by the renewing of your mind…"

The word *conformed* comes from the Greek word *suschematizo*, which means "to accommodate oneself to a model or pattern." Our English word *schematic* is a derivative. This verse is telling us that we should not allow our lives to be built according to the schematic or blueprint of the dark kingdom, but rather allow our minds to be renovated by the Holy Spirit, which will cause our transformation to become effective and operative. A person who has been spiritually transformed will never experience the power of that transformation until they have a different mindset.

When Moses led the children of Israel out of Egypt after many years of slavery, the Israelite people carried the slavery mentality with them. They were physically free from the oppression of Egypt and geographically separated from the land of bondage, but they were miserable and out-of-place because they were still slaves in their minds. Please understand, they did not think of themselves as slaves, but they thought as slaves. They viewed the world the way slaves view the world. Only two men, out of the masses, became freemen in their mindset and imagination. God's desire for the entire nation is spelled out in Exodus 19:5 and 6. He wanted to transform a bunch of slaves into a kingdom of priests; a royal race. But only two men and their families caught sight of God's transforming power and let go of their slave mentality. Two families out of thousands! The ratio is not much different today.

Called to Reign

The Bible, from beginning to end, is picturesque with God's design and plan for humanity.

He has always wanted his people to rule and reign with him. Think of it: man partnering with God, *created beings* co reigning with the Creator! God has always had loftier plans for our future than we've had for ourselves.

In the beginning, God created a beautiful world and put his created man in charge. Centuries later, he sent his Son to redeem us from the slavery of selfishness and give us authority over the kingdom of Satan. It has been ordained that Christ and his bride, which is his church, rule the universe for ever. Co reigning with God is not a new idea; it was his design from eternity.

2 Timothy 2:12 states that if we endure, we shall also reign with him. In 1 Peter 2:9, we are once again called a royal priesthood. Revelation 1:6 says that God has made us kings and priests. Revelation 5:10 also states that God has made us kings and priests, and we shall reign on the earth. In Revelation 20:4–6 John says, "And I saw thrones, and they sat on them, and judgment was committed to them…" Revelation 22:4–5 says, in reference to God's people, "…and they shall reign forever and ever."

These verses openly declare that God's ideal plan is for us, a bunch of ex-slaves, to begin thinking like freemen and experience the full transformation; become intimately familiar with the heart of God, and allow him to groom us for our ultimate purpose—to rule and reign with him as kings and priests!

Now, if we are to live throughout eternity, functioning in this capacity, then it is reasonable to conclude that we must prepare for it during this present phase of our existence. The life we now live is the dress rehearsal for the actual performance! Many live as if this life is the main event. It is not! It is the practice session for the main event.

For too long we have assumed that the *real* transformation of our lives would take place when Christ returns and we are gathered to him and that what we are here in this present life will not resemble what we shall be. This is certainly true in regard to quality of life, but not true at all relative to character, calling, and purpose. These must be developed now.

Does it not seem odd to think that a person could live a mediocre Christian life, never really rising above the slave mentality of this world, never practicing what they were called to do, and then, upon arriving in heaven become an instant expert in Godly judgment and righteous rulership? The truth of the matter is this: if we are not practicing Godly rule in our own sphere of influence, God will certainly not promote us to greater things. Unless we develop a kingly mentality here in this life, *we will not be a ruler in the kingdom to come.*

The Greek word for *king* is *basileus*, which means "the support of the people." Our English word *basis* is a derivative. The kingly mindset that we are to have is one of selfless leadership and prudent judgment. It carries the realization of responsibility toward those in our care. Certainly, there are those who use position and authority for personal gain and gratification. We call them tyrants. A king, in the truest meaning of the title, is one who has the interests of his people as his greatest concern.

A Kingly Mindset

> What my son? And what, son of my womb? And what, son of my vows? Do not give your strength to women, *nor your ways to that which destroys kings*. It is not for kings, O Lemuel, it is not for kings to drink wine, nor for princes intoxicating drink. Lest they forget the law and pervert the justice of all the afflicted. Give strong drink to him who is perishing, and wine to those who are bitter of heart. Let him drink and forget his poverty and remember his misery no more. Open your mouth, judge righteously, and plead the cause of the poor and needy.
>
> Proverbs 31:1–9 (NKJV, emphasis mine)

Proverbs chapter 31 not only describes the virtuous woman, but it first deals with the man of character. The advice in this passage comes from a queen mother to her son, King Lemuel, in the form of a warning against personal indulgence. He is urged to avoid giving himself to *that which destroys kings*. Those in leadership must have a clear, unmedicated mind in order to carry out their duties effectively. A leader does not refrain from indulgence simply because it is written somewhere in a rulebook. He exercises self-control because he is the support of the people and their well-being is top priority. It is here that kings and commoners are distinguished apart, not by birth, but by their mindset. A man of common thinking relies upon external restraints to maintain balance in his life. A king exercises self-control. A true free man is one who limits his own desires and governs himself out of an inner reservoir of wisdom. The commoner will ask, "Is it legal?" or "Is it a sin?" and if it is not technically wrong, he feels free to partake. His life is shaped and defined by an external law. The kingly minded will ask, "Is it prudent?" or "Is it wise?" He is far less interested in the lawfulness of a matter than he is in, whether or not, it is a good idea. There are things that are lawfully acceptable, but not very wise. The noble-minded are governed by an internal law that is constantly weighing the value of a matter based upon its long-range effects.

Proverbs 31:4–7 warns the king against intoxicating drink. In verses 4 and 5, King Lemuel's mother declares that it is *not for kings* to drink wine lest they forget the law and pervert justice. A king is in a position of tremendous influence, and therefore, whatever he indulges in will be felt by all those under his leadership. The king's mind must not be impaired by intoxicants, after all, why should he lend his faculties to another master? A common thinker will become defensive and say, "I have the right to partake," and while this is technically true, it speaks of selfishness and small-mindedness. Verses 6 and 7 indicate that wine is for the sick and dying and the one who needs a place of escape. So is it wrong to drink alcohol? That depends on who you are, a king or a commoner.

In the book of Titus, Paul the apostle admonishes the older men to be sober. The word sober comes from the Greek word *nephaleos*, which simply means "free from the influence of intoxicants." *Influence* is defined as "the power of persons or things to produce effects on others, especially by indirect means." (Funk & Wagnalls Standard Desk Dictionary) Paul is not saying, "Don't get drunk"; he is saying, "Don't be influenced by intoxicants." So the real question to ask, in regard to alcohol, is not, "How much can I drink without getting drunk?"; but rather, "Where should I draw the line in order to be absolutely free from its influence?"

The common thinking person will most always view freedom as the right to indulge, while the kingly minded person perceives freedom from the effects of indulgence, as true liberty.

Consumers versus Investors

Everything has a price, whether it is natural or supernatural. So life is about economics, the understanding of expenditure and gain. Even a good law system has, at its core, the idea of forbidding that which is ultimately "too costly" and promoting that which is prudent and beneficial.

The adage "everything is a trade-off" is used in reference to this universal concept. People calculate, on a daily basis, what is sufficient compensation for the time and effort given in a particular venture. In a wholesome economy, the cost of everything is adjusted according to how useful it is, how long it will last, and how badly people want it. The more value something has, the more you will have to pay in order to obtain it. It is then, very nearsighted, to decide against a good purchase simply because one cannot emotionally let go of the means. A wise man does not look only at the price to be paid, but also studies the value of the item to be purchased.

There are certain things that are considered priceless, and if they are indeed priceless, then whatever may be written on the price tag is certainly a bargain. A wise merchant is prepared to sell all that he has to purchase that which is priceless. This is the mentality of kings.

Since life is about economics, people are quite naturally found in one of two groupings: consumers or investors. Now, as we examine this more thoroughly, let us bear in mind that just because a consumer occasionally invests, this does not make him an investor; and just because an investor consumes a portion of his goods out of necessity, does not make him a consumer. We are studying a paradigm. A common thinking person will tend to have a consumer mentality while a person of prudence will be concerned with investments.

A commoner looks at the possessions and pleasures in his life and forms his identity accordingly. It is therefore, emotionally difficult for him to relinquish something at the present in order to gain something greater in the long run. Consumers tend to be focused on the immediate, while investors look beyond the present moment.

Observe the life of a commoner when a sum of money unexpectedly comes their way. Many times, amid paying legitimate bills, they will find an object of pleasure to buy; and sometimes, that object comes with a monthly payment. The commoner justifies this by saying, "Well, this money isn't enough to pay our debts anyway, so we might as well enjoy some of it." So instead of making every dollar take them closer to freedom, they go to town and buy a monthly payment! The expenditure that keeps on spending! Their life was certainly better off before the extra money came to them. Spending is the mindset of the poor, not the wealthy.

It is in their emotional identity to consume their wealth, and the sooner, the better. The life of a commoner is defined by what he has at the moment, and that thought pattern usually sabotages his future.

The kingly minded, however, are not afraid to give up a desire, postpone a pleasure, or tighten their belt financially in order to purchase greater things in the future. A farmer, for example, holds in his hand the edible portion of his crop. Some of it will feed his family and some will be held back for next year's planting. Now, I realize that the modern concept of farming is to sell your entire crop, pay some of last year's debt, take out a loan for next years seed, and hope and pray for a good harvest so you can do it all over again. It just goes to show that common consumer thinking is widely accepted, and we *all* must rise above it.

A farmer with an investor mindset can raise a crop and feed his family and smile because his seed for next year is safely stored. He can live free from debt because God created plants to reproduce their own seed.

When a consumer is encouraged to invest, it makes him sad because his money was already emotionally spent. The one thing going through his mind, is the fact that he should refrain from spending a portion of his money, and since money is made to consume, any portion of it that is *not* consumed is providing no pleasure and is, therefore, lost.

An investor views time and money as seeds to be strategically planted. He gets excited at the thought of his resources multiplying. He does not feel a loss when he finds an investment opportunity because he is already feeling the wealth of return.

A Christian with a kingly mindset does not view his abstinence from fleshly indulgences as a loss of freedom, but realizes that a sacrifice made in this life is an investment in the life to come, and the dividends will be greater than he can possibly imagine. A king knows that the self-imposed restraints that he lives by, are literally purchasing great reward in the kingdom of God. Living as a king should live in this present world, is an invaluable rehearsal for kingly reign in the world to come. The truly wise recognize the kingdom of God to be priceless, and are willing to pay any price to enter in.

Righteous Judgment

"Don't Judge!" This has been taught in Christendom for years. The secular world is also sold on the idea that we should not judge anyone. The scripture that is usually cited is Matthew 7: 1, 2: "Judge not, that you be not judged. For with what judgment you judge, you will be judged; and with the measure you use, it will be measured back to you."

This passage does not command us to refrain from judging others, as much as it reveals the way judgment actually works. In practical application, it is impossible to abstain from judging.

Consider this example. If you meet someone for the first time and mentally profile them according to the way you perceive them and decide that they are not worthy of your friendship, you have judged them. But what if they strike you in a positive manner, and you decide that they are a person of honesty and good character? Have you not judged them? Of course you have, only, no one is upset when you judge favorably. Judgment goes both ways: for *and* against. So God has not commanded us *not* to judge, but he has taught us how to do it righteously. John 7:24 (NKJV) says, "Do not judge according to appearance, but judge with righteous judgment."

In order to judge perfectly, one must have all the facts. A wise judge will probe past a surface impression in order to find out what is at the root.

The Apostle Paul sternly admonishes the Corinthian church members to settle their own disputes rather than to stand before an unsaved judge. He reminds them that they will judge angels in the kingdom to come, so they should be intentionally focused on the development of that skill.

"I say this to your shame. Is it so, that there is not a wise man among you, not even one, who will be able to judge between his brethren?" (1 Corinthians 6:5, NKJV).

If we are to rule and reign with Christ in his kingdom, then judgment is going to be a large part of what we do. It is absolutely necessary to learn how to do it righteously.

> You will know them by their fruits. Do men gather grapes from thornbushes or figs from thistles? Even so, every good tree bears good fruit, but a bad tree bears bad fruit. A good tree cannot bear bad fruit, nor can a bad tree bear good fruit. Every tree that does not bear good fruit is cut down and thrown into the fire. Therefore by their fruits you will know them.
>
> Matthew 7:16–20 (NKJV)

It isn't hard to accurately determine the species of a tree when you can see the fruit on its branches. By the same token, it is not difficult to judge the character of a person when the fruit of their life is obvious. However, a person should not be judged entirely by a single incident, but by observing their life over the course of time. We must remember that the measuring rod we use to judge others will be the one used to judge us. We have a tendency to judge others by the cold hard facts and judge ourselves according to our intentions. A good judge cannot hold a double standard.

"For if we would judge ourselves, we would not be judged" (1 Corinthians 11:31, NKJV).

The perfect place to begin is in our own personal lives. If we learn how to cooperate with the Holy Spirit in the judgment and refinement of ourselves, we would learn to rely upon his discernment in all matters.

God is the perfect judge because he knows the entire truth about every situation. Judging with righteous judgment consists of relying upon the voice of God to tell us what is at the heart of a matter, and not making a surface assessment. It is our destiny to co rule an ever-expanding kingdom with Christ. It is time to practice!

The Desire to Be Great

> Then a dispute arose among them as to which of them would be greatest. And Jesus, perceiving the thought of their heart, took a little child and set him by Him, and said to them, "Whoever receives this little child in My name receives Me; and whoever receives Me, receives Him Who sent Me. For he who is least among you all will be great."
>
> Luke 9:46–48 (NKJV)

Some of Jesus' disciples seemed to desire a position of importance in the kingdom of God, but a dispute had arisen among them as to which would be the greatest of all. This was apparently something that they tried to keep from Jesus's attention; after all, it did seem rather childish. But Jesus perceives their thoughts and with an ironic gesture, draws a small child to himself in illustration. He then gives a very short lesson on humility.

Now, I am sure that we've all heard sermons on this passage, pointing out the wrongness of the disciples' desire to be great and the virtue of humility. The conclusion that we seem to always reach is that any desire to be great should be squelched, and humility should be chosen instead. However, a closer look at this passage reveals that Jesus did *not* chide them for desiring greatness, but rather in a few words, told them how to achieve it!

This particular discussion seems to be tabled for a while, but then resurfaces at the Last Supper just a few hours before the crucifixion.

> Now there was also a dispute among them, as to which of them should be considered the greatest. And He said to them, "The kings of the Gentiles exercise lordship over them, and those who exercise authority over them are called 'benefactors'. But not so among you; on the contrary, he who is greatest among you, let him be as the younger, and he who governs as he who serves. For who is greater, he who sits at the table? Yet I am among you as the One who serves."
>
> Luke 22:24–27 (NKJV)

Jesus now spends more time explaining the concept that they had obviously missed earlier. He again does not scold them for their desire to be great, but carefully explains that they are going about it the wrong way.

The common idea of greatness is associated with the CEO, the man in charge, the president, or the king. The most visible people in the highest positions are considered great. But Jesus declares that things are just the opposite in his kingdom. The one who desires to be great should have a servant's heart. Making the choice to serve others with no ulterior motive actually paves the way to exaltation.

Jesus was once again telling them *how* to be great. He was saying, in essence, "I am great; my kingdom is great, everything I create is great. I was the one who put the desire for greatness in you. I designed and destined you to rule and reign with me. I need great people. I am developing people of greatness, but you cannot be truly great in my kingdom by using the common philosophy, so I am going to explain to you the secret of true greatness. Begin to serve others. Encourage them, honor them, and help them succeed. Push them to the top. Help them become all they can be. This is the attitude of kings, for they are the support of the people."

Jesus then gives his disciples a glimpse into their own future in the next three verses!

> "But you are those who have continued with Me in My trials. And I bestow upon you a kingdom, just as My Father bestowed one upon Me. That you may eat and drink at My table in My kingdom, and sit on thrones judging the twelve tribes of Israel."
>
> Luke 22:28–30 (NKJV)

I can only imagine the stunned silence and the sense of awe that engulfed them as the impact of Jesus's words began to be felt. Jesus had just revealed to them *their ultimate purpose for eternity*!

He *did* want them to desire greatness in his kingdom! They were destined to be great, but now, it was no longer a competitive argument between them. *They would each sit on a throne and judge a tribe of Israel!* The thought of it was staggering! Perhaps they were thinking, "Who am I to sit on a throne and have a position of rulership over one of Jacob's sons and all of his descendants?" Yet, Jesus had said it, and furthermore, had shown them how to do it! The key is humility. Not the false humility that refuses to accept what God's word says about you, but the true humility that simply agrees with God, regardless of anyone else's opinion. Nowhere in the Scriptures are we warned to avoid greatness. The Scriptures do, however, instruct us over and over how to be great. In Ephesians 4:1–3, we are told that in order to walk worthy of God's call, there are certain character qualities that must be developed. The first one on the list is humility. The Greek word that is used here means lowliness of mind, a sense of moral insignificance, and a humble attitude of unselfish concern for the welfare of others. The word was unknown in classical nonbiblical Greek because the revolutionary paradox of becoming great by choosing lowliness was original with Christ (The Complete Word Study Dictionary).

Consider for a moment the fact that Jesus Christ, the God of the ages, stooped to the level of humanity, and then allowed himself to be rejected and executed by humanity. Another example of humility and greatness is found earlier in Christ's ministry when he began to wash his disciples' feet. One of them pulled away because it just didn't seem right. Common practice dictates that a master should be served, not subjected to the ignoble task of serving. But Jesus broke the rules of common protocol with his perfect humility. He is the King of the universe who exemplified his greatness through service.

Do What Kings Do

> Therefore, since we are receiving a kingdom
> which cannot be shaken, let us have grace,
> by which we may serve God acceptably with
> reverence and Godly fear.
>
> Hebrews 12:28 (NKJV)

What kind of people are qualified to have an unshakeable kingdom entrusted to them? Unshakeable people! People who have taken their stand upon God's unshakeable word and decided that they will be the king that God is looking for. A kingly nature is never developed by common living. It is a matter of choice. Your life may have been characterized by mediocrity until this moment. But now, you have heard the call, and it is time to rise. No matter how ordinary or insignificant you may believe yourself to be, give your belief system to God because he specializes in taking the ordinary and using it extraordinarily.

I believe the mark of excellence that characterizes God's kingdom should be found in the lives of his followers. So if you are a king, then do what kings do!

A Covenant Kingdom

*C*ovenant.

Here is a word that is seldom used by the majority of the modern church and even less understood. The mental image of a mountain man and an Indian cutting their wrists, ceremonially binding their arms together and becoming blood brothers is quite revolting to a more civilized society. The ultra civilized people, however, who reject the heathenistic concept of mingling blood, never grasp the beauty that lies within the covenant itself. As we lift the core concept of blood covenant out of the manmade ritualistic barbarism, we will see that it originated with God.

We are compelled to examine the idea of covenant because the Scriptures are a record of God's covenants with mankind. We must view the Scriptures through the lens of covenant, if an adequate understanding of it is to be gained. Why is covenant necessary? Why can't God simply do what he wants on the earth, whether or not a covenant exists? To answer these questions, we must go back to the beginning.

God created everything and owns everything to this day. The Bible says, in Psalm 24:1 (NKJV), "The earth is the Lord's, and all its fullness, the world and those who dwell therein."

But even though God owns the world, he does not have access into it, except through covenant. In the beginning, God placed the whole earth under the jurisdiction and authority of man until the Day of the Lord. If the seven day week, in which six days belong to man but the seventh day belongs to the Lord, is a symbol of God's plan for the earth, then six thousand years belong to man, but the seven thousandth year belongs to God. This seventh day is referred to as the Day of the Lord. This means man makes the decisions on earth for six thousand years, and then, it goes back under God's direct control.

Any person who owns rental property understands this concept. You can own the rental, but have no access until the lessor invites you in. When the contract expires, the lessor moves out, and you the owner, have hands-on control once again.

Mankind is the official manager of the earth, and anyone who is not a bona fide human being must enter by permission. So God went looking for someone to cut a covenant with in order to have a doorway into the earth. Ultimately, God *became* human so that permanent access into the earth could be established.

The redemptive purchase of Jesus Christ on the cross was a product of covenant, as well as an inauguration of covenant. All of God's connectivity with man since Eden has been through the doorway of covenant. Covenants are all about access.

The Hebrew word for covenant, *berith*, meaning "compact, pledge, treaty, and agreement" comes from the primitive root word *barah*, which carries the idea of cutting. From ancient times, a covenant was a solemn oath that was ratified by the ceremonial cutting of flesh and shedding of blood. The seal of blood signified several things. First of all, the fact that a covenant was dissolvable only by the death of one of the covenant partners, was symbolized by the ceremonial cutting. Secondly, if the covenant should be broken on either side, the penalty was the shedding of blood, resulting in their death. The consequence for breaking one's covenantal word has always been death. This penalty could extend to the third or fourth generation, if necessary, because the effects of broken covenant are usually *felt* to the third and fourth generation. The ceremonial shedding of blood also indicated the solemnity of the compact between the two parties. Each was saying to the other, "I am pledging my very life to you." The scar that remained in each of their bodies was a constant reminder that their sacred oath had been given. Covenant people were "marked" for life and lived within the boundaries and provisions of that agreement.

The power that exists within a covenant is attributed to God, due to the fact that he is the legal witness to the pledge. His blessing is invoked upon the keeping of the covenant, as well as a terrible curse naturally resting upon those who disallow it. When covenants are made, God is recognized as the creator of it and, therefore, the one who presides over it.

Covenants are reciprocal in nature. When one partner places a legitimate demand upon the covenant, the other partner is obligated to satisfy that request.

After the demand has been satisfied, then they are free from that particular debt and also able to place a demand of their own.

Covenant versus Contract

A covenant and a contract are similar only in the fact that they are an agreement between parties. Their many differences do not permit them to be used interchangeably. A covenant has, for its foundation, the integrity of the individuals and their spoken word, whereas a contract stands upon the integrity of the facts. If a contractual agreement is found to contain fraudulent information or be formed around the intent to defraud, then that contract is immediately considered void and nonbinding.

A covenant is founded upon the honor of the words given in pledge.

Contracts are legal agreements; covenants are *sacred* agreements. Contracts are basically designed to hold someone to their word and are, therefore, based upon distrust. In a covenant, however, each party declares their promise, which is founded upon their own faithfulness of character.

The Power of Covenant

In Joshua chapter 9, we find the nation of Israel coming back into their homeland under the leadership of Joshua, Moses' successor. About four hundred years prior to this, a unique set of circumstances had taken them down into Egypt to live. After a time, the

Egyptians had overcome them and enslaved them, and it was during this period that squatters had moved in and established an unlawful claim on Israel's territory.

Now freed from Egyptian bondage, they are faced with reconquering their own land. God was giving them instruction and strategy in their conquest, and one specific command forbade them to enter into covenant with any of the foreign people groups that they were supposed to expel. Shortly into their reclamation effort, a tribe of people from the region of Gibeah devised a plan to deceive Israel. The Gibeonites were very fearful of Israel and knew for certain that Israel's God was fighting their battles and no one would be able to withstand him. So they sent a delegation dressed in ragged clothing, wearing worn out shoes, and carrying dry moldy bread.

> And they went to Joshua, to the camp at Gilgal, and said to him and to the men of Israel, "We have come from a far country; now therefore, make a covenant with us." Then the men of Israel said to the Hivites, "Perhaps you dwell among us; so how can we make covenant with you? So they said to him: From a very far country your servants have come, because of the name of the Lord your God; for we have heard of His fame."
>
> Joshua 9:6–9 (NKJV)

The Gibeonite men convinced the leadership of Israel that their clothes and shoes had been new when they started their journey, and the bread had been taken hot out of the oven the day of their departure. Israel believes their story, cuts a covenant with them guaranteeing their safety and sends them on their way. A few days later, Israel discovers that the Gibeonites live a very short distance away; they have been tricked!

Although the people of Gibeah had deceived them, the covenant remained because of the integrity of Israel's word.

> Then all the rulers said to all the congregation, "We have sworn to them by the Lord God of Israel; now therefore, we may not touch them. This we will do to them: We will let them live, lest wrath be upon us because of the oath which we swore to them."
>
> Joshua 9:19, 20 (NKJV)

The covenant between Israel and Gibeah was *not* the plan of God, but now, nothing can be done to change it. There are no loopholes in a covenant. No one can cry, "Foul!" No one gets a do-over. The covenant stands based upon the premise that Israel's word is honorable, even if the word of the Gibeonites is not, and God Almighty is presiding over it.

Five hundred years later, King David is enquiring of God concerning a three-year famine that has plagued the land. God's reply to David in 2 Samuel 21:1 shows the unchangeableness of covenant. "It is because of Saul and his bloodthirsty house, because he killed the Gibeonites." So David calls in representatives of the remaining Gibeonites and asks what can be done to make atonement for Israel's breach of covenant. They ask for seven of Saul's descendants to be given to them, so David brings seven of Saul's grandchildren to the Gibeonites. These seven are executed, and after that, God heeded Israel's prayers for rain.

This illustration of the power of covenant is astounding! We can see that covenant stands because a sacred oath was given, not because all the facts were in order. We can also see that God himself was invoked as witness and party to this covenant, and five hundred years later, he was still watching over it! A covenant that *should not have been made in the first place* still had incredible power five hundred years later!

Covenant versus Sovereignty

In our modern American culture, we hear much more about the sovereignty of God than we do about our covenant God. A fully sovereign God can do anything he wants to, whenever he wants to do it, without answering to anyone. Much of our modern theology is laced with the belief that God does things because he is the biggest. Whenever something unexplainable happens in our lives, we simply chalk it up to the sovereignty of God.

It is very difficult, however, to discern the nature of a sovereign God because whatever he chooses to do, is consistent with his character. If he smiles on the unjust or pours calamity on the just, it is simply explained as the sovereignty of God. Some have alleged that he can put sickness and disease upon his children in order to teach them or refine them, and that the devil may bring forth a miracle in order to deceive. Neither of these suppositions are within the realm of possibility. How can God do bad things to bring about good? How can his children know so little about him?

It is certainly true that God makes decisions out of his own wisdom and has no accountability, but when this point becomes the fulcrum in our theology, we present to the world a God who cannot be understood. I am not accusing our clergymen of malicious intent; I am quite sure that in an attempt to help their parishioners through difficult times, God's sovereignty was offered as the answer to their questions. It may have been the easiest answer, but it was certainly the wrong answer!

God is a covenant God, and his word reveals to us over and over that he does *nothing* outside the boundaries of covenant. When God entered into covenant with man, his sovereignty became a non-issue. Sovereignty means "having supreme authority and being free from outside influence." But true sovereignty can only be preserved if one never enters into an agreement. It is impossible to make a choice without eliminating other choices. Sovereigns have the power to make any choice they wish, but their sovereignty is diminished when even one choice is made.

If, for example, you entered your local automobile dealership and looked at each and every one of their cars, you are not bound in anyway *until* you sign on the proverbial 'dotted line'. You are sovereign *until* you enter a contractual agreement to pay off the car over time. When the contract is signed, you have become indebted and obligated in an area of your life that once was sovereign. It is not possible to enter into a binding agreement and manage to keep all of your options open. So it is with God. In his sovereignty, he made a covenant with a man named Abram and promised him a son and declared that through that son would spring forth a mighty nation of people and, eventually, Messiah himself! After his word was given to Abram, God was no longer sovereign in this matter. He had traded sovereignty for covenant. God cannot enter into a compact with someone while somehow retaining the option of ignoring his promise. This is an absurdity.

We are told in Hebrews 11:6 that it is not possible to please God without faith. But how can you have faith in a God who may, or may not, honor his word? The "sovereignty of God" philosophy undermines faith because it suggests that God is not obligated to us in any way, effectively nullifying his promise. Nobody is going to have faith in someone who can make a promise without any obligation to keep it! Consider again the example of Abraham (his name was changed by God in Genesis 17) on his way to the mountains of Moriah to sacrifice his son on an altar at the commandment of the Lord. The Scriptures tell us in Genesis 22:1 that this was a test. But this was not merely a test of Abraham's character and obedience, it was, on a much deeper level, a test of Abraham's understanding of covenant and confidence in his covenant partner. The covenant that God had made with him was unprecedented in the fact that it extended to every descendant of Abraham and, ultimately, to everyone who would call upon the name of the Lord. God was not going to enter into a covenant of this proportion with just anyone! The plan of redemption rested on this covenant!

The covenant-cutting ceremony had taken place almost fifty years before. God had come to Abram, as he was then called, and instructed him to select a three-year-old heifer, a three-year-old female goat, a three-year-old ram, a turtle dove, and a young pigeon. He was to divide the animals into two pieces down the middle, and lay each piece opposite the other on the ground. The two birds were not cut, but laid on opposite sides. Then, in what is perhaps the most amazing covenant-cutting ceremony in history, God himself, in the visible form of a smoking oven and burning torch, comes down and passes between the animal pieces. The covenantal significance of this is overwhelming! God Almighty had literally *indentured* himself to a mortal man by covenanting to do certain things in Abram's life and in the lives of his descendants!

A covenant-cutting ceremony of this kind may not have been particularly uncommon, in that each party would declare their contributions and responsibilities to the other and walk between the cut flesh of the animals, thus signifying that what had been done to the animals would be done to them if this covenant should ever be broken. But *this* covenant was extraordinary because it was between God and human, Creator and creation, Perfection and imperfection! God had bound *himself* with a divine oath to a *man* and staked his very existence on it! Furthermore, Abram was not required to contribute to this covenant nor stake his life for its validity. God did not require Abram to pass between the animal flesh.

So now as Abraham nears the place of sacrifice with his strapping young son, he tells his servants to wait at the base of the mountain because he and his son would go further and sacrifice and then they *both* would return. How could Abraham be so sure? Because God's existence depended on it! He did not know how every detail would play out, but he did know the outcome. He was not sure if God would stop him from carrying out this grisly task or if God would raise up Isaac his son, from the ashes, but it really didn't matter because God had said that Abraham's posterity would begin in Isaac, and so he *and his son* would be going home together.

Abraham's faith in this story has been admired and extolled for thousands of years, and rightfully so, but Abraham was not functioning on "blind" faith. He knew that he had a covenant with God, and it was not possible for God to change his mind and take his son. This is faith, and faith lives in the heart of a covenant-minded person.

Had Abraham been thinking about the sovereignty of God, his instructions to his servants may have sounded like this, "All right, fellas. I want you to camp here at the foot of the mountain, and I want you to really pray because I don't know if Isaac is coming back with me or not. God is sovereign and he can do what he wants, so if Isaac is sacrificed, then, I don't know what we'll do. God's ways are higher than our ways, so we really don't know how it will turn out. We'll just have to trust God." Now, these words may seem noble and pious, but there is a conspicuous presence of worry and a glaring lack of faith. Blind trust in God is *not* faith. It may perhaps be called loyalty, which is good and necessary, but it can *never* be called faith. True faith is never blind. The God-kind of faith is the ability to "see" the invisible and firmly grasp hold of it. Jesus said, in John 6:40 (NKJV, emphasis mine), "Everyone who *sees* the Son and believes in Him may have everlasting life."

Abraham's faith was certainly not blind. He knew *what* was going to happen; he just didn't know *how* it would happen.

So Isaac and his father left the camp and traveled farther up the mountain, carrying the wood and the instruments of sacrifice; but no animal. Isaac, who was about twenty-five years old, questioned his father about this, and Abraham replied, "My son, God will provide for himself the lamb for a burnt offering." What an amazing prophetic utterance! Abraham knew that he was obligated to sacrifice his only son because his covenant partner had asked for it. But he also knew that if Isaac died under the sacrificial knife, he would stand before God with his obligation fulfilled, and he would be able to place a demand upon their covenant. I can imagine Abraham, lifting his tear-stained face toward heaven and saying, "I have fulfilled the demand that you placed upon our covenant, and now I am free to place a demand upon it: *Raise him up!*"

God is greatly pleased with that kind of faith, and he did stop Abraham before Isaac was harmed. He also supplied a sacrificial animal for Abraham and Isaac that day. I firmly believe that God wanted Isaac to see how stable and irrevocable the covenant was, because after his father's death, the covenant would be his.

Let us now consider Job. Job thought it was within the character of God to kill righteous people along with the evil. He said in Job 9:22, 23, "It is all one thing: Therefore I say, 'He destroys the blameless and the wicked.' If the scourge slays suddenly, He laughs at the plight of the innocent."

Conversely, Abraham, in his negotiation with God concerning Sodom and Gomorrah, declares that God *cannot* destroy the righteous with the unrighteous.

> "Suppose there were fifty righteous within the city; would You also destroy the place and not spare it for the fifty righteous that were in it? Far be it from You to do such a thing as this, to slay the righteous with the wicked, far be it from You! Shall not the Judge of all the earth do right?"
>
> Genesis 18:24, 25 (NKJV)

Abraham declared the *righteousness* of God because he knew him within the framework of covenant. Job asserted the *sovereignty* of God, although a covenant of protection for him and his family had been offered to him. Abraham had unwavering faith in the covenant that existed between he and God, whereas, Job lived as though God can break his promises, and found himself on the *outside* of a perfectly good covenant of protection.

Whether or not a person has faith in their covenant is evidenced by their speech.

Abraham said, matter-of-factly, "*We* will come back to you" (Genesis 22: 5b), but Job said, "For the thing I greatly feared has come upon me, and what I dreaded has happened to me" (Job 3: 25, NKJV).

God the Father looked upon Job the way that he looks upon all of his children—focused more on their strengths than on their weaknesses. He was well aware of the fear and worry in Job's heart. He also knew that Job had a faulty understanding of covenant and, in all practicality, lived as though he didn't have one. But God boasts of Job's devotion and exalts his integrity and character.

Some people have the mistaken idea that Job did everything right, and that God, by calling him a man of integrity, was sanctioning every part of Job's life. God doesn't do that to *anyone*. He calls him a blameless and upright man, but never calls him a man of faith. Job's integrity is exemplary, but that does not mean we are to emulate the faithlessness in Job's life. Job is just like every one of God's people, he had strengths, and he had areas of weakness. God knew that when the dust had finally settled; Job would not only be a man of unswerving devotion, but also a man who lived by the word of God, no longer controlled by fear.

Job saw God through the philosophy of sovereignty: God can do what he wants; he can do good or evil, give and then take it all away. He's bigger than the rest of us, so who's gonna call him on it.

To the casual onlooker, this may appear humble; but in reality, this attitude contains an inherent arrogance that bows reverently to a sovereign who is obviously unjust, making us look pretty good while God is painted the villain.

Sovereignty-minded people also view God as having hands-on control of everything; therefore, whatever happens must be his doing. They forget that while the earth is the Lord's, it is under man's authority until the Day of the Lord.

> "The earth is given into the hand of the wicked. He covers the faces of its judges. If it is not He, *who else could it be?*"
>
> Job 9:24 (NKJV, emphasis mine)

This is incredible! Job apparently believed that God is the cause of everything that happens, and did not realize that it was *Satan* who attacked him!

I have seen this philosophy at work in the church today, and the enemy simply loves it! Satan can pillage and plunder his way through people's lives, and they will—either in fatalistic resignation, continue to serve God, or they will turn a bitter face toward him and disavow any allegiance. The enemy really likes both reactions, because in both cases, God is blamed, and he walks free to do it over and over again.

Sovereignty-minded people usually do not exercise spiritual authority over Satan because they don't seem to see him as the problem, and if God is truly sovereign, then, all authority is vested in him only.

Job believed two basic lies:

1. Everything that happened to him was the perfect will and purpose of God.
2. God can provide a hedge of protection, and then arbitrarily remove it. Job never really believed that he and his family were under God's divine protection. We know this because Job acted as if he didn't have much faith in it.

> And his sons would go and feast in their houses, each on his appointed day, and would send and invite their three sisters to eat and drink with them. So it was when the days of feasting had run their course that Job would send and sanctify them, and he would rise early in the morning and offer burnt offerings according to the number of them all. For Job said, "It may be that my sons have sinned and cursed God in their hearts." *Thus did Job regularly.*
>
> Job 1:4, 5 (NKJV, emphasis mine)

Job acted as if God's hedge of protection was inadequate. He was controlled by fear and worry. He would offer sacrifices of appeasement to God, *just in case* his children had sinned. He did not know for sure that they had sinned, but he felt that they may not be safe from judgment, unless he did something about it. How that must have grieved the heart of God! But things are no different today. People have a copy of the covenant word of God lying on their table, which says that heaven and earth will pass away before God's word passes away, and they still insist on a contingency in case God's word fails. All we need is plan A: God's covenant word. If you have a plan B, be prepared to use it, because plan A is neutralized by your faithlessness in it. Faith is how you are connected to the covenant; unbelief is how you disconnect.

God did not remove the hedge of protection. Job had already disconnected and estranged himself from it through worry, fear, and unbelief! God did not break or remove the covenant, he simply revealed to Satan that Job was in his power.

The book of Job largely contains the discourse of Job and four friends who came to encourage and exhort him in his calamity. Three of the men affirm that Job has sinned against God; otherwise, these things would not have happened. God was not happy with them because this was not true. Job defends his uprightness, but alleges that God can afflict a righteous man without cause. This also is not true. The fourth man, Elihu, condemns self-righteousness and defends God's goodness.

> "Behold, God is mighty, but despises no one;
> He is mighty in strength of understanding.
> He does not preserve the life of the wicked,
> but gives justice to the oppressed. He does not
> withdraw His eyes from the righteous; but they
> are on the throne with kings, for He has seated
> them forever, and they are exalted… As for the
> Almighty, we cannot find Him; He is excellent
> in power, in judgment and abundant justice; *He
> does not oppress.*"
>
> Job 36:5–7 (NKJV, emphasis mine)

Elihu declares that God's character will not allow Him to oppress the righteous. Then, he points out the magnificent inalterability of God's Word.

> "Listen to this, O Job; stand still and consider
> the wondrous works of God. Do you know
> when God dispatches them, and causes the
> light of His cloud to shine? Do you know how
> the clouds are balanced, those wondrous works
> of Him who is perfect in knowledge?"
>
> Job 37:14–16 (NKJV)

Elihu is the only man, out of the four, that God does not sternly rebuke, and God's own words when he speaks to Job out of a whirlwind in chapter 38, are very similar to Elihus's words.

> "Where were you when I laid the foundations of the earth? Tell Me, if you have understanding. Who determined its measurements? Surely you know! Or who stretched the line upon it?...Now prepare yourself like a man; I will question you, and you shall answer Me: Would you indeed annul My judgment? Would you condemn Me that you may be justified?..."
>
> Job 38:4, 5; 40:7, 8 (NKJV)

God was sick and tired of being misrepresented and declared, essentially, that the word that framed the wonders of the universe, created the marvels of nature, and maintains everything in balance and beauty is the *same word* that spoke the hedge of protection into being! The existence of the universe, including God himself, hangs upon the validity of his word! If God says you have a hedge of protection, then you've got a hedge of protection, and do not act as if you don't!

When God is finished speaking, Job, very humbly says, "I had heard of You [only] by the hearing of the ear, but now my [spiritual] eye sees You. Therefore I loathe [my words] and abhor myself and repent in dust and ashes" (Job 42:5, 6, Amplified Bible).

What did Job repent of? Unbelief. God had given him his word, and if Job had stood on it and acted as if he had a covenant, the enemy would not have had access into his affairs.

Abraham's faith was accounted to him for righteousness, whereas, Job was required to *repent* of his unbelief in God's word. Job would have sounded a lot like Abraham if he had said, "Today my children are feasting, but nothing can harm them because God's word has formed a hedge of protection around me and my family, and we are protected!"

Many people today also seem to forget the all important fact, that the account of Job's life predates the cross, when Satan could legally and legitimately accuse us before God. The sin of all mankind had been merely covered by the atoning sacrifices of the Old Covenant, but never actually removed. When Jesus Christ went to the cross as the perfect sacrifice, he *removed* our sin as far as the east is from the west, and left Satan standing disarmed and beaten. Jesus said, in John 12:31, just before his crucifixion, "*Now* is the judgment of this world; *now* the ruler of this world will be cast out." Satan can no longer accuse us to God. Calvary changed everything! He has no legal charge to bring against us, since Jesus bore our penalty and removed our judgment. The only weapon in Satan's arsenal is deception; nothing else exists for him.

So many Christians act as if God can violate his word and still be called good, and considered honest. One of the most disrespectful things you can do to a person of long-standing godly character, is treat them as if they might go back on their word at any moment, for any reason. God gets this type of treatment everyday! There is no faith in this way of thinking. All the variableness is transferred to God and we can walk around free of all responsibility because no matter the outcome, we can chalk it up to God's sovereignty. If we pray for a person's physical healing and they get worse and die, we can say that God, in his sovereignty, chose not to heal them, and we don't have to even consider the fact that there are several obstacles to receiving answers to prayer, *and they are not in heaven, they're all down here!*

We have allowed experience, or the lack of it, to shape our theology instead of going to the word and saying, "God, when you healed us all at Calvary, you eliminated the option of 'choosing not to heal' later on. We know that you do not lie or make mistakes, so the failure is on our part. We prayed for our friend and they grew worse and died. Will you reveal to us why we failed to receive the healing?" This is a truly humble prayer, and God will answer it. It is only reasonable to conclude that all discrepancies are found on our part instead of laying the failure at the feet of a perfect God and walking away as if we had done everything just right. This is an unspeakable arrogance, which has blinded our eyes and limited our redemption.

Sovereignty in History

Many of the Europeans who first settled in this country brought with them a paradigm of despotism in spite of their best efforts to escape it. People are more disposed to do what they are trained to do, even if they despise the results.

The indigenous people who welcomed them had a great understanding of covenant, as most tribal families do. So it is not surprising that the native clans entered into treaties with the European people so that peaceful coexistence could be established. The pilgrims who landed at Plymouth were quite possibly the only covenant-minded immigrants during those early years of American settlement. Before their feet touched land, they made a covenant with God and each other, known to us as the Mayflower Compact. But many more of European descent believed that even though they had entered into a binding agreement, they still retained the option of changing their minds. And they did change their minds over and over until the treaties were broken, and the indigenous people had been brutally exploited. This is the type of "freedom" that had been modeled in Europe for centuries, and so it was deeply rooted in their belief system. They hated being exploited by cruel overlords, so they came to America, never really abandoning despotism, but rather, becoming the despot.

So the Christianity that was brought to this continent was, in many cases, tainted by this ungodly mindset. The native Americans understood the integrity of a person's word, and had the gospel of Jesus Christ been presented to them as a covenant between God and man; I believe they would have accepted Christ, en masse. But instead, they saw the Europeans who claimed to represent God, make an agreement and then arbitrarily change the terms as if they were still sovereign.

And so approximately five hundred years later, we are still plagued by a non-covenant mentality in the church, even though the Scriptures we claim to know so well are all about covenant.

We, as a nation, are now living under the curse of broken covenant. Everything that was done to the native tribes, —from the murdering of their infants to the theft of their land, from the stripping of dignity and freedom to the addiction of man-made substances, is now being done to us—we are paying a great price.

Living as Gentiles

In Matthew chapter 6, Jesus admonishes us over and over, not to worry. He doesn't encourage us to *try our best* not to worry because worry isn't a good idea; he made it very clear that we are not to worry. He says in Matthew 6:31, 32, "Therefore do not worry, saying, 'What shall we eat?' or 'What shall we drink?' or 'What shall we wear?' For after all these things the Gentiles seek. For your heavenly Father knows that you need all these things."

Let us look more closely at the phrase "for after all these things the Gentiles seek" because the covenant language here is unmistakable. When it comes to covenant with God, there are only two groups of people in the world: those within covenant and those without. In the days of Jesus's earthly ministry, the covenantal line was drawn between Jews and Gentiles, Jews being the insiders. The nation of Israel set great store by the fact that they were blood descendants of Abraham, God's covenant partner, and that, by virtue of pedigree, they inherited God's covenantal blessings. Those who were born outside the nation of Israel were simply on the outside of God's family and without any hope. Jesus, however, taught that nationality and pedigree did not, in any way, connect a person to the covenant. Since Abraham connected to God's covenant by faith, his descendants would also have to connect by faith. The connection is, and always has been, faith.

But in Matthew 6: 32, Jesus uses the phrase "for after all these things the Gentiles seek" to drive home an all important point. We could also read the phrase this way, "For after all these things *non-covenant* people seek." His audience consisted primarily of Israeli covenant people, and so the message they were hearing was this, "Do not live as though you have no covenant with God. Non-covenant people worry about life because they are on their own with no loving, caring Father to provide for them. But covenant people who have worry and stress in their lives are living as though they are not in covenant with God, the ultimate provider. They are not only displeasing God, but are essentially without a covenant. Remember Job? He had a covenant, but lived as though he didn't, and the result was that he found himself on the *outside* of God's protection. Many Christians have the same mistaken idea that Israel had; that pedigree is more important than faith. They settle back on the fact that they have prayed a prayer and asked Jesus Christ to forgive them and be their Savior and now that they are *born* into God's family, and God is their Father, the covenant is theirs no matter what they do from that point forward. The Apostle Paul uses an olive tree metaphor in Romans 11 to illustrate exactly what it takes to be connected to the kingdom of God. He shows us clearly that Jews and Gentiles alike are attached by faith and disconnected through unbelief.

So, successful, day to day, Christian living is not entirely dependant on a once-uttered prayer. It comes from a heart that gives preeminence to the covenant word of God and aligns its own words and actions with it. Having a covenant, but living in fear and worry, has exactly the same net result as, *not having a covenant at all*!

Everything Is Made of Words

Then God said, "Let there be light"; and there was light.

Genesis 1:3 (NKJV)

In the beginning was the Word, and the Word was with God, and the Word was God. He was in the beginning with God. All things were made through Him, and without Him nothing was made that was made.

John 1:1–3 (NKJV)

Jesus *is* the Word of God! This amazing revelation had completely reshaped the way John understood God, and we also must grasp it in order to even begin understanding covenant. Our human mind struggles with the idea that Jesus is eternally existent due to the emphasis placed upon his title: Son of God. John 3:16 states that God gave his *only begotten son*, thus, proving that Jesus came forth from him, and yet, there is no mother involved, and Jesus has no beginning or end. The Father-Son analogy can only becomes clear when we realize that Jesus is the *Word* of God. It is not hard to believe that if God the Father is eternal, then his ability to speak words is also eternal. There has never been a moment when words were not a part of God's existence. Now, we begin to understand *how* Jesus was begotten of God. *He came out of God's mouth!*

We must not insist upon squeezing the relationship of Jesus and his Father into our tiny human concept of reproduction. The Father-Son analogy is given to bear out only one truth: Jesus came out of God. Let all natural reasoning stop here. If Jesus is indeed the word of God, then he has always existed in God and did come out of God—out of his mouth. God *spoke* to a virgin girl named Mary, and she humbly received it and the words became seed in her womb. A new body began to develop within her for those words to live in.

"And the Word became flesh, and dwelt among us" (John 1:14, NKJV).

The word translated *begotten*, later in this passage, as well as John 3: 16, is the Greek word *monogenes*, which means "the only one of the family," and when used in reference to Christ, speaks of his relationship with God.

The Greek word *teknon*, which means "child or offspring," is never used by God in regard to Jesus or by Jesus in regard to himself, which would indicate a literal birth or beginning. Christ reveals himself as having always been in the Father's heart and mind and coming forth from God's mouth to create a universe consisting of the micro and the magna. What holds the electrons in orbit around the nucleus? The word of God. What holds planets in their astronomical orbits? The word of God. Everything that was made was first a word in the mouth of God. *Everything* is made of words.

Covenant of Words

"Do you take this woman to be your lawful wedded wife?" It was November 21, 1998, and I was marrying René Marie McNeel. At one point in the ceremony, I escorted her to a small low table upon which was a piece of bread and a goblet of fresh grape juice. We knelt on opposite sides, and as beautiful music gently filled the room, I began to speak to only her. I told her again of my ideals, goals, and vision for the future; I assured her of my devotion to God and my decision to love, lead, and care for her.

After many things had been spoken, I took a portion of the bread and tore it in two. As I offered her a piece, I asked her to be flesh of my flesh in the body of Christ. I then drank from the cup, offered it to René and asked if she was willing to partake of my life in the life of Christ, and follow me as I follow God. As she lifted the cup to her lips, she was covenanting with me in the sight of God and human witnesses to be my closest companion in life, taking upon herself my name, my mission, and my purpose. We were joined together by words. Covenants are made of words.

We live in a culture that has not placed value upon words, and consequently, in many urban areas, language has been reduced to primitive grunts and gestures. The state educational system has used the abysmal sight-reading method for many years, and statistics have shown the reduction in literacy. Satan perverts the use and meaning of words and works tirelessly to promote lies and broken promises, destroying peoples' faith in other people and in God.

All of these things have worked to neutralize the effectiveness of God's covenant word to us. The enemy, having failed in his attempt to destroy the written word, now targets the individual person. Whether they find reading difficult and don't enjoy it, or are simply too busy or too tired to read, the net result is the same—people are not really reading God's covenant word!

People cannot live in the blessings of covenant, if they don't know anything about it!

Words are primarily creative, secondarily communicative. At creation, God gave man the ability to express the imaginations of his heart. Words were given as a tool, powerful enough to take the hidden thoughts of one's mind and bring them into reality. Words are an audible substance of our innermost character, projected into the open. But as everyone knows, whoever controls the man controls his creativity, and whatever is found in his heart will come out in his art. When the integrity of man is compromised, the power of his promise is lost.

We are, perhaps, the most marketed-to society in history. We are inundated with cheap words, drowning in slogans and sales-strategies. Many of the ones putting forth these words are not really interested in the truthfulness of them, but rather, their effectiveness. The misuse of words and the subversion of truth in marketing seems to be justified by how many consumers can be sold on an idea. Too often, success is measured in dollars and cents, instead of a legacy of Godly character.

God has given us his immutable, unchangeable, unalterable word!

> "God is not a man, that He should lie, nor a son of man, that He should repent. Has He said, and will He not do? Or has He spoken, and will He not make it good?"
>
> Numbers 23:19 (NKJV)

God is not like us. He does not give his word and then change his mind. We must not measure the character of God by our past experiences with people. It is a tragedy for us to view God through the lens of fallen humanity. You can trust God! The word of God created the universe, and that word has come to us, as a divine covenant.

Casual Covenants

> "For by your words you will be justified, and by your words you will be condemned."
>
> Matthew 12:37 (NKJV)

Many good people today have wondered why they seem to live under a cloud of misfortune. While there are several things that can cause this, perhaps the first area of suspect is our daily speech. For many, a close examination will reveal that they have *casually* made covenant with bad luck, disaster, disease, etc., by adhering to the belief that words are really inconsequential. The Scriptures, however, draw a parallel between the human tongue and a ship's rudder. James 3:4 and 5 reveals the principle that the tongue is the "steering wheel" of our lives. It would be absurd to turn the steering wheel of your car to the left, while moving forward, but fully expect the car to turn right. It is also absurd to speak bad luck, but somehow expect to live under a blessing. Now there are those who deny this truth and argue that they have said many things that did not come to be. I am not suggesting that every glibly spoken word suddenly plays out in reality no more than a sudden jerk of the wheel instantly turns a ship in a different direction. Ships are steered by *holding the rudder* at the desired pitch until it comes about. Our lives are steered by *consistently speaking* certain things. Winners do not talk like losers, and losers do not talk like winners. Words are not impotent. The words we speak will activate the forces of light or the forces of darkness. Words grant jurisdiction, and the king of each kingdom is waiting for permission to be granted him by our words to carry out his plan in our lives. A casual covenant is just as binding as a ceremonially sealed agreement. Remember the complaining words of the nation of Israel? The more a person talks about dying in the wilderness, the more likely they are to die in the wilderness. Each kingdom, whether good or evil, wins in your life by a vote of one. You and I cast the winning ballot everyday with our words.

Kingdom Authority

> Then God said, "Let Us make man in Our Likeness; let them have dominion over the fish of the sea, over the birds of the air, and over the cattle, over all the earth and over every creeping thing that creeps on the earth."
>
> Genesis 1:26 (NKJV)

In the very first verse of the Scriptures that refer to mankind, God establishes two things:

1. Man was to be made in the image and likeness of God.
2. In order to truly resemble God, man must necessarily have dominion over every living thing on the earth.

It was in God's original plan for man to be the authority figure in the earth. As we have already discussed in a previous chapter, man forfeited his righteousness and came under the lawlessness of the fallen angel, Lucifer. Man still retained a certain level of authority, but now it was largely at Satan's disposal.

The human family lived under the law system of sin and death.

Fast forward now, approximately four thousand years, and we find Christ walking in the authority of the first Adam. Born without the corrupt spiritual DNA of Lucifer, he simply lived and moved as Adam and Eve had done prior to the fall. This, however, was completely foreign to the rest of the human race. Jesus's closest friends were utterly amazed when he calmed a windstorm with his words, caused a fish with two coins in its mouth to be the first one that Peter caught, rode an unbroken donkey, multiplied food, walked on water, performed miracles of healing and restoration, and acted as if this were perfectly normal! But Jesus did not come to "wow" us with a grand display of power; he came with a plan. He came with *the* plan. The plan to raise mankind from the dead and reunite him with his creator, so that the goodness of God could flow through man's God-given authority on the earth.

The Authority of Mankind

Without a doubt, all true authority is vested in Christ Jesus. First Peter 3:22 tells us that he is at the right hand of God and that angels, authorities, and powers are subject to him. Jesus himself said in Matthew 28:18, "All authority has been given to Me in heaven and on earth." As a matter of fact, Jesus Christ was the only one, since the fall of man, to possess authority over Satan. He alone held the keys of the kingdom. Things were different now than they had been at the beginning. The keys of managerial authority had been given unreservedly to Adam, and he had walked in dominion over the whole earth. Everything obeyed him. He was subservient to no one, except God. But when Adam obeyed Satan, his spirit died within him and he was separated from the presence of his creator. Mankind was now in the grip of a cruel overlord who would manipulate him in inconceivable ways in order to use and exploit his managerial power. *Nothingness* was the prize of this new administration, and all humans would now be filled with it. Once flooded with the life of God, now ironically enough, man existed in the absence of it, and no matter how long his life span or how vast his possessions, he was doomed to an eternity of emptiness and void once he drew his final breath—unless, of course, a sinless human being could be born.

The Perfect Man

> But when the fullness of the time had come, God sent forth his Son, born of a woman, born under the law, to redeem those who were under the law that we might receive the adoption as sons.
>
> Galatians 4:4, 5 (NKJV)

Jesus Christ, the perfect Man. His mother was human; his father is God. It was the only legal way to dethrone Lucifer and reestablish the kingdom of God on earth. As a legitimate member of the human race, he could exercise authority. As incorruptible God, he could never be subservient to anyone. But the plan of God was far more complex than anyone could have anticipated, and when it was fully accomplished, Satan found himself in a permanent predicament. He, in his zeal to eliminate Christ, had made a horrible legal error; he had managed to have Jesus—the only human *not* guilty of sin— executed. But Jesus was also divine, so his death served as payment for everyone else's guilt, opening up a door of redemption and reconciliation to God. Anyone who accepts Jesus Christ as Savior, Redeemer, and Lord can walk in authority over Satan.

Colossians 1:13 (brackets mine) says, "He has delivered us from the power [authority] of darkness, and conveyed us into the kingdom of the Son of His love." The authority of the first Adam is vested in the second Adam, which is Christ; so anyone who is one with Christ in Spirit, has access to his authority."

> And you are complete in Him, Who is the Head of all principality and power.
>
> Colossians 2: 10 (NKJV)

Authority in the Earth

> All authority has been given to Me in heaven and on earth. Go therefore and make disciples of all the nations.
>
> Matthew 28:18b–19a (NKJV)

> Behold, I give you the authority to trample on serpents and scorpions, and over all the power of the enemy, and nothing shall by any means hurt you.
>
> Luke 10:19 (NKJV)

Jesus is declaring plainly, in these verses, that anyone who is connected to him in spirit can and should walk in the authority that the first Adam forfeited. Those who are found in Christ have true dominion over the earth.

Jesus is now seated at the right hand of God. The human body that was born of Mary is not on the earth, but his spiritual body *is* on the earth—his body of believers. The authority that God delegated to mankind in Eden has once again been vested in the human being. We have heard it said that Satan is the god of this world, and it was assumed that his power was so terrible that a Christian's only hope for survival was to avoid making a commotion large enough to draw his attention. The truth is that *both* God Almighty *and* Lucifer must have permission from a legal citizen of planet earth, in order to perform their activities here. Mankind is the legal authority on earth. The Scriptures do refer to Satan as the "god of this age" in 2 Corinthians 4:4, but Ephesians 1:20–23 declares that Christ Jesus is authoritatively seated above *everything*. So what does this mean? First, let me briefly explain one universal concept: the one who creates something retains jurisdiction over that creation. Consider the words of Jesus to the religious leaders when he was asked whether or not it was lawful to pay taxes to Caesar. He said, "Show Me the tax money." So they brought him a denarius. And he said to them, "Whose image and inscription is this?" They said to him, "Caesar's," and he said to them, "Render therefore to Caesar the things that are Caesar's, and to God the things that are God's" (Matthew 22:19–21, NKJV).

Simply stated, "If the money in your pocket was created by Caesar's financial system, then you must follow his rules, because ultimately that money belongs to him—he created it." Consider a modern example: a young couple, wishing to marry, purchases a marriage license from their state. They do not tear their eyes away from one another long enough to read the fine print, which varies slightly from state to state, but in essence declares that their union and *everything produced by it, is under the jurisdiction of the state.* A few years later, after the family has grown, the state steps in, takes their children and places them in foster care because the Christian parents dared discipline them according to the biblical model. As the story spreads around the country, good people become indignant. "How can this happen in a free country? What is happening to our freedom?"

The answer is very simple. The young couple asked the state to create their marriage and preside over it. The representative of the state who officiated at the wedding declared for all to hear, "By the power vested in me by the state of—, I pronounce you man and wife." If the state creates the marriage, then legally, the state has jurisdiction over it. No one should be surprised at this. Sometimes, the words "what God has joined together, let not man put asunder" are wrongfully used in the ceremony. God wasn't the One who joined this couple. The presiding authority is emanating from the state capitol, not God. We also know that it is not possible to be created by *two different* entities. Jurisdiction is retained by only *one*; this is why the Bible says, "No servant can serve two masters" (Luke 16: 13, NKJV). The correct legal statement should be, "What the state has joined together, the state may, at its discretion, take apart." *The creator of something retains jurisdiction over it.*

Now let us return to 2 Corinthians 4:4 in light of this concept. Satan is the god of the *empire* he created, *not* of the earth itself. The world's system of money and trade are Satan's design. Nowhere in the Scriptures does God declare ownership of the commercial structure. In fact, God warns his people to come out of the world's system because it is destined to incur his wrath and judgment. The bottom line is this: the only authority that Satan really possesses has been given to him through an alliance with the human being. Man collaborates with the enemy and helps build his insidious empire based upon the promise of wealth and power. But as we have already discovered, man gives his authority to Satan and gets Satan's 'nothingness' in return. It is the ultimate scam.

Civil Authority

At this point, it becomes necessary to address a very misunderstood subject—civil authority. Romans 13:1 says, "Let every soul be subject to the governing authorities. For there is no authority except from God, and the authorities that exist are appointed by God."

This verse tells us that *all true authority* comes from God. The problem found in the modern church is not necessarily the interpretation of this Scripture, but in the application of it.

At the time this scripture was written, the authoritative chain of command was understood to start with God as supreme, and then flow down to the monarch, king, or emperor. From there, authority was delegated in decreasing degree to military officers and civil magistrates. At the very bottom of this chain was the populace who were predisposed to accept and obey what was handed down as law. When the Apostle Paul penned these words in AD 56, he was not suggesting that everyone who *claimed* to have authority was to be obeyed. He describes the characteristics of God-given authority in verse 3 when he says, "For rulers are not a terror to good works, but to evil."

Now, there are those who usurp authority. Are they to be obeyed? Certainly not! When good people obey an illegitimate authority figure, they are *not* obeying the scriptural mandate found in Romans 13. We have developed such an aversion to rebellion that we tend to obey every authoritative voice, whether it is legitimate or not.

In order to correctly apply the command to obey authority, one must first determine *who* that authority is. As an American, I must know the structure of authority in America.

When fifty-five delegates from twelve states met in Philadelphia in 1787 to draft our nation's Constitution, something took place that had never happened before. Perhaps for the first time in the history of mankind—a government was established upon the recognition that God had granted freedom to every human being. Therefore, the United States Constitution recognizes true authority as vested in the populace, *not in a government*. Our constitution does *not* grant rights, for then the people would draw their freedom from the writers of it. No, the constitution only *recognizes* the inherent freedoms that God vested in every human life, and declares that those God-given, unalienable rights cannot be taken away by anyone else.

Every public office is staffed by a public servant, from the county sheriff, to the president of the United States; they all are allowed to serve at the *discretion of the people*. If at any time, a publicly elected official rises up and uses delegated authority for personal gain or injustice, that servant has gone rogue and forfeited their position. That is called a usurpation of authority, and the people who delegated that authority are in no way bound to tolerate it, much less, obey it! Illegitimate authority gets its power when gullible people obey it.

We must realize that within the scope of human existence on this planet, a constitutional republic form of government is a very new idea preceded by several millennia of "king-on-top, people-on-the-bottom" empires, and the "monarch" mentality quite unwilling to change. Now, here we are, more than 225 years later, with a vast majority of our citizenry completely convinced that the president is the supreme authority in our land, the people are at the bottom and are somehow morally obligated to obey whatever our government passes into law. This is a travesty!

The American citizen is the supreme authority in this country, under God.

Before every election, candidates parade before us, trying to convince us to give them some of our authority. Then, those elected officials enact laws that enslave the very people who gave them a job, while we in religious circles perpetuate this madness by telling our people to submit to their *servants*.

If a grounds keeper at a large corporate headquarters building walked into the CEO's office and began ordering him or her to pay large amounts of money in order to remain the CEO. It would be mere minutes before security showed up and the problem would be handled.

In the United States of America, the county sheriff, the president, and everyone in between are "grounds-keepers." You and I are the CEO. The citizen is at the *top* of the authoritative chain, and every public servant finds their place of support, somewhere *under* the citizen. The only way this can be legally altered is by contract in which the citizen trades unalienable (God-given) rights for civil (government created) rights. Freedom always comes from God. Civil rights are manmade and just another name for slavery.

Exousia

The predominate Greek word in the New Testament for "authority" is *exousia*, which means "permission, authority, having the right to act." Let us look again at the first few words of Luke 10: 19, "Behold I give you the authority to trample on serpents and scorpions…"

Jesus Christ is here delegating authority to his disciples. This authority extends over all the power of the enemy. This is the same authority that Jesus possessed.

Over the years, I have come across several books on spiritual warfare. Some of them were out in left field and some were, at least, a bit closer to the truth. Most of them had the followers of Christ trading punches with the devil, being hit with demonic artillery, and literally running themselves to the ragged edge in their attempts to push back the dark kingdom. Jesus Christ, from whom our authority comes, did none of these things. He cast out demons with *a word*. On one particular occasion, a woman came to him on behalf of her demon-possessed daughter. Jesus told her that her need had been met, and upon returning home, she found her daughter free of the demons that had been tormenting her. Jesus did not go to her house or even see her daughter! That is spiritual warfare! As I studied this subject a little further, I began to realize what Godly authority looks like. The word *exousia*, as we stated earlier, means "having the right to act." The root from which it comes is *exesti*, which denotes authority that *does not acknowledge the presence of a hindrance*. This is the authority that Jesus was talking about in Luke 10: 19! This is the authority that is vested in the church!

Jesus simply went through his day-to-day ministry as if there were no devil. He carried out the instructions of his Father without a backward glance. Jesus lived and ministered as though opposition did not exist! He never told his disciples, "Well, boys, we need to pray about our trip to Jerusalem because we will encounter tremendous demonic opposition. We've got to be ready because Satan will try to defeat us." No! No! No! He just went where he needed to go! We must understand that when we look Satan in the eye and acknowledge him as an adversary, we grant him a certain amount of power. He is a *totally powerless* being who waits for the one with authority to look him in the eye and admit that he is a force to be reckoned with. *He is empowered by our acknowledgment of him.* Some will certainly argue, "You can't just ignore him, after all he has *some* power." Yes, he has some power; he received it from you when you recognized him as an enemy to be dealt with. Please do not misunderstand me. I am not suggesting that we be ignorant of how our enemy thinks and schemes. I firmly believe we must know how he operates. In fact, the Scriptures tell us that if we do not, he will take advantage of us. What I am saying here, is that his power is *deception*, not strength! Many Christians shrink from their calling because they are afraid of confronting the devil in order to fulfill it. We were not commissioned to confront the devil; we were commissioned to advance the kingdom! Jesus stripped Satan of all authority and reduced him to nothing at the cross. We cannot allow a fear of opposition control our effectiveness for God. We must simply be about our Father's business.

Upon this Rock I Will Build My Church

What is the true form and function of the church? Is the church just a building? Is it the people? Is it both?

Many questions have been asked in regard to the church and its true purpose. God has provided all of the answers in his word.

First, let us examine the word that is translated *church* in the Scriptures. It comes from the Greek word *ecclesia*, and is first referenced in Matthew 16: 18, "... and on this rock I will build My church, and the gates of Hades shall not prevail against it."

The word *ecclesia* (ek-lay-see'-uh) comes from *eccaleo*, "to call out"; thus, *ecclesia* is an assembly of the called ones. The word was borrowed from secular Greek and describes a legal assembly of people or delegates and was used in reference to the Roman senate. While *ecclesia* primarily denotes a legal assembly of people, it does not exclude the building being used for meeting. Tertullian, (AD 150–AD 220) wrote of ecclesia as a building used for meeting. Clement of Alexandria, a contemporary of Tertullian, mentioned the double meaning of the word.

So what was Jesus saying in Matthew 16: 18 when he said that he would build his church? If we insert the definition of *ecclesia* into the verse, it would read this way, "and on this rock I will build My *law-making body*, and the gates of Hades shall not prevail against it." Jesus is talking about his followers seated in a legal assembly, exercising their God-given authority and establishing kingdom rule upon the earth. This is all about God's governmental plan—the advance of his kingdom. For too long, we have asked the wrong questions, which always lead to the wrong answers—for example, "Do I have to go to church to be a Christian?" to which the usual answer is, no. Now, I suspect that this question was designed to bring us to the answer that we wanted to hear, so let's ask a more honest question. "Now that

I am part of Christ's body, should I find my place and function in his church? The answer is certainly, yes. If the church is a spiritual senate designed to establish kingdom order in the earth, then, I must find my seat. The concept of *going* to church or *attending* church must be superseded by the vision of a legal gathering of the called ones, authoritatively seated, conducting kingdom business for the glory of the king!

I remember a few years ago, I was praying with a couple in my office about a particular matter. During the prayer, I quoted Matthew 18:19 to officially declare the power of our agreement: "Again I say to you that if two of you agree on earth concerning anything that they ask, it will be done for them by My Father in heaven."

Suddenly, it was revealed to me by the Spirit that this verse is describing a *legal quorum*. If two people agree on a matter that is consistent with the counsel of the Holy Spirit, they have just established *kingdom law* on the earth with regard to that particular matter. Every spiritual being, whether angelic or demonic, is immediately apprised of the new authoritative measure and must conduct themselves with respect to it. The only way for this law to be annulled is for the humans who established it, to change their declaration.

The church that Jesus is building will worship the King, grow into the measure of Christ, determine spiritual climate, speak the will of God into manifestation, make his enemies his footstool, and be everything that Christ is looking for in a wife. Let's find our place and get in it!

Find Your Proper Seat

Then David dwelt in the stronghold, and called it the City of David.

2 Samuel 5: 9 (NKJV)

The word *dwelt* comes from the Hebrew *yoshev*, which, not only means "to dwell, live or settle," but also means "to establish your authoritative seat or position." It has to do with one coming into his own; stepping into one's ultimate purpose and destiny. This word also occurs in Psalm 133:1, "Behold, how good and how pleasant it is, for brethren to dwell together in unity!"

We generally use this verse to center attention on the need for unity within the church, and while this is certainly crucial, I believe its impact is weakened unless we focus on the word *dwell* in conjunction with the word *unity*. The message of this scripture is this: how wonderful it is when God's people discover their purpose, step into their anointed calling, find their proper seat, and work harmoniously with the other members of this spiritual senate. Verses 2 and 3 of Psalm 133 compare this kingdom ideal with the precious anointing oil that was poured out on Aaron's head when he was commissioned for his priestly service and with the dew of Hermon descending upon the mountains of Zion. But the last sentence is the most revealing:

For there the Lord commanded the blessing-
Life forevermore.

(Psalm 133: 3b)

A casual reading might cause us to merely conclude that the Lord was in that particular place when he commanded the blessing; however, the blessing was spoken over Mt. Gerezim, and it was also believed that the blessing of the covenant symbolically, if not literally, resided there. We can see in light of this that the blessing is not only spoken *from* a specific place; it is also spoken *upon* a specific place. It is my belief that Psalm 133 is speaking prophetically of the Day of Pentecost. In Luke 24:49, Jesus said, "Behold, I send the Promise of My Father upon you; but *tarry* in the city of Jerusalem until you are endued with power from on high."

The word translated *tarry* is the Greek word *kathizo*, which carries essentially the same meaning as the Hebrew word *yoshev*, "to make to sit down, to set, appoint, to be seated in one's proper place." Christ instructed his disciples to go to Jerusalem, find their proper place, be established in that place, and be unified in mind and purpose for *in that specific place*, the Holy Spirit would descend. It is not about *waiting*; it's about being in one's proper place. For too long, the posture of the church has been that of waiting on God to move, but the truth has always been that God is waiting on his followers to be properly seated and unified. We must recognize the principle here: Jesus told his disciples *where* the Holy Spirit would be poured out, not *upon whom*. The anointing of God flows down upon divinely appointed offices; then, he calls people into those positions. If the called ones step into their proper place, they find that the anointing to function in that calling is already there.

It has been mistakenly believed that *people* are authenticated by the anointing on their lives, but the demonstration of power through the anointing of the Holy Spirit has always validated the word of God, not necessarily the messenger.

> And they [the disciples] went out and preached everywhere, the Lord working with them and *confirming the word* through the accompanying signs, Amen.
>
> Mark 16:20 (NKJV, emphasis & brackets mine)

Many ministers have made the terrible mistake of assuming that God was sanctioning their personal lives because the anointing flowed through them when they functioned in their calling. *God does not authenticate our personal lives with his anointing. He anoints his authentic offices,* and it becomes our personal responsibility to yield our character to the management of the Holy Spirit. As Dr. Ronald Cottle once said, "The saddle and bridle of integrity must harness the horse of your anointing." The anointing that rests upon your calling must be exercised within the framework of Godly character.

Let us look again at the ministry of Christ.

> And He was handed the book of the prophet Isaiah. And when He had opened the book, He found the place where it was written: "The Spirit of the Lord is upon Me, because He has anointed Me to preach the gospel to the poor; He has sent Me to heal the brokenhearted, to proclaim liberty to the captives and recovery of sight to the blind, to set at liberty those who

are oppressed; to proclaim the acceptable year of
the Lord." Then He closed the book, and gave it
back to the attendant and *sat down* [kathizo; in
His proper place of authority and purpose]. And
the eyes of all who were in the synagogue were
fixed on Him. And He began to say to them,
"Today this scripture is fulfilled in your hearing."

Luke 4:17–21 (NKJV, emphasis & brackets mine)

Jesus read a description of Messiah from the book
of Isaiah, after which he seated himself in the chair that
was reserved for Messiah. Then, and only then, did he
declare himself to be the Messiah. It is interesting to
note that verse 21 says, "And He *began* to say to them…",
Jesus would say much more from his seat of Messianic
authority before his earthly ministry was finished.

Jesus Christ was also the anointed Teacher of the
kingdom. In Matthew 5:1, we find these words, "And
seeing the multitudes, He went up on a mountain, and
when He was *seated* [kathizo; proper seat of calling and
authority] His disciples came to Him."

Before our Lord ever gave his inspired Sermon on
the Mount, he sat down. Yes, he probably found a nice
comfortable place on the grassy hillside to sit down,
but when he was seated, he was also officially accepting
the role of teacher, and from that seat, he had the right
to speak authoritatively about his Father's kingdom. In
Ephesians 1:20b, 21, the apostle Paul states that God
"seated Him [Christ] at His right hand in the heavenly
places, far above all principality and power and might
and dominion, and every name that is named, not only
in this age but also in that which is to come."

I get very excited every time I read this passage, because here we see Jesus officially and forever seated [kathizo; His proper seat of destiny] as King of Kings and Lord of Lords! He is above everything that has, or will ever have, a name!

Ephesians 2:6 says that we have been made to "sit together in the heavenly places in Christ Jesus." We have been *positionally* seated with Christ in heavenly places! If we use that authority as good stewards, we will overcome and sit with him *experientially*!

> To him who overcomes I will grant to sit with Me on My throne, as I also overcame and sat down with My Father on His Throne.
>
> Revelation 3: 21 (NKJV)

We must find our proper, God-ordained place in Christ and operate in the anointing that flows there, knowing that ultimately we are destined to sit with Christ on his throne!

God's offices and callings are anointed. There is a waterfall of blessing that flows down on each position. He is calling us to yield ourselves to his will and step into our purpose and destiny. The ultimate place of contribution and fulfillment is in the place God has called us to be. So many people treat their giftings and callings as sidelines with 'making a living' as the mainline. They aim at financial security first, and then when they are old, realize that they majored on the minor and never fulfilled their purpose on earth. God called us to live, not make a living. The waterfall that flows down on your proper seat, contains your living, and those who make their life completely about his kingdom, are in the place of greatest blessing. God has already ordered everything pertaining to life and godliness to flow down upon your proper seat in his kingdom, so don't get sidetracked, seek first the kingdom, find your divinely ordered seat of destiny and purpose, and sit down under the waterfall of kingdom fullness!

No Spirit of Timidity!

> For God has not given us a spirit of fear, but of power, and of love and of a sound mind.
>
> 2 Timothy 1:7 (NKJV)

During a word study of this verse, a startling truth was revealed to me. The word *fear* in this instance should have been translated "timidity" or "cowardice."

"For God has not given us a spirit of cowardice..." I remember questioning God about this, after all, timidity is a legitimate personality trait, right? The Lord began to show me, first of all, that timidity does not find its origin in the kingdom of God. Secondly, timidity cannot *exist inside* the kingdom of God. This was somewhat frightening to me because an element of timidity had always been present within my introverted personality. As I began to search and study, I started to realize that the God of all dominion had created mankind to have dominion. *The kingdom of God is a kingdom of dominion.* As we learned previously, Godly authority does not recognize the presence of a hindrance; thus, Godly authority is the antithesis of timidity!

But he said to them, "Why are you so *fearful* [timid]? How is it that you have *no faith*? (Mark 4:40, NKJV, emphasis & brackets mine)

In questioning his disciples, Jesus acknowledges the connection between 'timidity' and 'no faith'. I followed this word, in its various forms, and came to Revelation 21:8 which says, "But the *cowardly*, unbelieving, abominable, murderers, sexually immoral, sorcerers, idolaters, and all liars shall have their part in the lake which burns with fire and brimstone, which is the second death."

This is staggering! Timidity is listed in company with the most heinous of sins, and finds its ultimate end in hell! I, again, meekly questioned this new revelation and immediately sensed God's answer. Timidity is no more compatible with the kingdom of God than lying, murder, or sexual immorality. Timid people will never exercise the authority delegated to them, just as the servant who received one talent shrank from his responsibility and was condemned for it. Timidity is a product of self-consciousness, which, of course, is rooted in self-centeredness and is quite willing to place a low emotional assessment of itself over the advance of the kingdom. God's kingdom is filled with leaders, rulers, kings, and priests; there is simply no place for cowardice.

The latter part of 2 Timothy 1:7, tells us what God *has* given us:

1. Power (*dunamis*, which carries the idea of ability)
2. Love (*agape*, the essence of God himself)
3. A sound mind (*sophronismos*, a combination of *sos*, "safe" and *phren*, "the mind," hence, safe-

thinking. The word denotes good judgment, disciplined thought patterns, and the ability to understand and make right decisions.)

Timidity and cowardice generally emanate from the emotional sphere of our soul. God has equipped us to overcome this by relying upon the dynamic power of the Holy Spirit; the love of God, which has been poured into our hearts; and a healthy mind filled with good judgment and self-discipline.

Kingdom Distribution

So why is kingdom authority such a big issue? Why is it so important that we exercise that authority? The answer is simple: the kingdom of God cannot advance on the earth without it. Christ's perfect government is carried abroad by our feet and distributed by our hands. That's right. The kingdom of God is carried throughout the world by the *only ones* qualified to do it—you and me. Remember, the only legal authority on earth until the Day of the Lord, is the human citizen. If we do not distribute the essence of our King, it will not be distributed. Some will certainly argue with this and say, "God can move sovereignly if he chooses. We are hearing reports from all over the world, of God's power reaching out to remote people groups through dreams and visions, in regions where there is not a representative of Christ."

My answer to this is based upon the word of God, not what I see or think I see, in the world around me. God does *not* move sovereignly, he moves covenantally!

If he is speaking to unreached people groups in miraculous ways, it is because he commissioned some of his covenant people to pray, and they granted him access through prayer. God does not break moral law! Somebody, somewhere, invited God to intervene in the earth. This is the power of intercessory prayer: God and man partnering to reach the world. If you see God moving in power and might, don't assume that he is doing it sovereignly. The doorway into that area was opened through prayer long before the outworking of power was visible.

The concept of kingdom distribution is so important, that Jesus illustrated it on two separate occasions, and when a message is given twice in the Scriptures, the astute pay particular attention.

In Matthew 10, Jesus calls his twelve disciples to himself and commissions them to go ahead of him into certain cities, proclaiming the kingdom and performing kingdom works. He gave them power [*exousia*, "authority"] over sickness, disease, death, and demons and said, "...freely you have received, freely give." This was a very important step in the development of those chosen men. They had been given kingdom authority and were fully expected to exercise it. Luke 9:6 says, "So they departed and went through the towns, preaching the gospel and healing everywhere."

Sometime later, after John the Baptist had been executed, Jesus and his disciples went into a deserted region to rest. But a multitude of people searched him out and came to him. Jesus saw them and was moved with compassion, so he began to heal their sick. When evening came, the disciples suggested that the crowd be dismissed so they could go into the villages and buy food before nightfall. Jesus simply turns to these previously empowered men who have healed the sick, cast out demons, and seen miracles of provision at their own hand, and says, "They do not need to go away. *You* give them something to eat."

The disciples did what many disciples are prone to do—they forgot about the *spiritual authority* that had been given them and took an assessment of their *physical resources*. Jesus did not chide them, but rather, stepped in and took over. He took the small lunch of five loaves and two small fish that a young lad had presented, blessed it, broke it into pieces, and gave it to his disciples to distribute. Jesus's followers ultimately fed five thousand men—beside women and children—and then gathered twelve baskets full of leftovers.

This miracle is literally a snapshot of the kingdom of God from Calvary to the return of Christ.

Even though the disciples had pulled up short when asked to feed the multitude, the picture is very clear: Jesus would not have asked them to perform this miracle if they were not able to do it. God does not set people up for a fall! The disciples could have said, "Master, why don't you sit down and rest. You've been ministering all day, and you're very tired. We've got this one." The truth is, they did possess the authority to perform this miracle, but fear and natural thinking got in the way.

Jesus did step forward as the leader, but it had already been determined that this miracle must be done at the hands of the disciples. After Jesus had blessed the food, I can see Jesus dropping a small piece of bread and a small chunk of fish into each disciple's hand, and pointing them toward the multitude. As they began to move toward the seated crowd, perhaps, they were thinking, "This little morsel of food will not fill the first person I come to, but I'll do what Jesus says, and when I run out of food, I'll just go back and tell him. I'm sure he'll come up with something."

As each disciple tore a small piece and gave it to the first person, they realized that the portion in their hand was not any smaller. They went to the second person, then to the third, and on and on. I can imagine them looking out over the crowd and catching the eye of a fellow disciple. An unspoken message flashed from one to the other, "It is happening in *my hand*!"

The miracle of kingdom distribution *always* happens in the hands of God's people!

As I read through this amazing historical account one day, God asked me a question, "What was Jesus doing while his disciples distributed bread and fish?" As I paused to think about this, he answered his own question. "He was sitting down." The spiritual revelation hit me hard and fast. Jesus *is* the blessed bread of life. He had been broken symbolically at the last supper and *placed in each disciple's hand*; he had been literally broken when he was scourged and crucified.

That day on the shores of Galilee, Jesus painted a portrait of the kingdom of God! He blessed and broke the bread at the evening hour, knowing that he would be completely sacrificed at the evening hour. He placed the bread and fish in each disciple's hand, knowing that the *power* of the cross would be placed in the hands of every disciple. Then he *sat down and waited* for his disciples to distribute food to every single person, knowing that after his resurrection, he would *sit down* at the right hand of his Father and *wait* until his followers bring the bread of heaven to every person.

Suddenly, it became clear to me: the church has not understood its place in the kingdom enterprise! When Christians see the need for a miracle in someone's life, they typically ask God to *come and bring it*, or somehow send it. When it doesn't happen, something is said about God's sovereign will, and the truth of the matter gets lost. God is *sitting down*. He *will not bring anything*. It is not his job! The answer is already in the hands of his people waiting for distribution! He is waiting. Waiting for what? Waiting for us to hand out the bread and fish and make his enemies his footstool!

Jesus established this truth a second time when he fed the four thousand. This miracle was identical to the first one in form and illustration. God was making sure that we would get the picture.

It is very interesting to note that the feeding of the five thousand is the *only* miracle recorded in *all four* gospels. And in John's account, it is also recorded that on the day after the feeding of the five thousand, Jesus publically declared himself to be the Bread of Life.

Here is the conclusion of the matter: the Bread of Life has been torn and placed in our hands. If the people of this world partake of this Bread, it will be because we gave it to them. It is neither proper nor profitable to ask God to distribute kingdom provision when it is in our hand.

Authoritative Declaration

The subject and study of authoritative declaration could easily fill a volume of its own, so my intended purpose here is to focus on its general description and basic purpose. Let me begin by stating that authoritative declaration is *not* prayer. Prayer is essentially dialogue with God, and it would be absurd to exercise authority toward him, neither would it be proper. During times of prayer, however, I have been instructed by the Holy Spirit to declare an authoritative word into a particular situation. Authoritative declaration is aimed at obstacles and adversaries, *never* God. Many Christians, due to a lack of understanding, simply refrain from making bold declarations. Some opt instead to pray and ask God to do things that he cannot rightfully do. Remember, we are the ones with the authority in the earth, so in order to advance the kingdom, we must get the mind of God in all matters, and then declare his will into the situation. The Scriptures tell us in several places that Jesus would often find a quiet place to commune with his Father: this is prayer. The Scriptures also tell us that he would rebuke a demon spirit with a word or speak healing to a diseased individual; this is authoritative declaration. Jesus, when encountering the sick, never asked his Father to reach down and touch them. No, he had already prayed, so he knew his Father's will. He had been sent to heal, save, and deliver, so it was his responsibility to declare kingdom benefit into the lives of people.

In Acts chapter 3, we read of Peter and John approaching the temple at the hour of prayer and healing a lame man who daily sat at the gate begging for money. Peter's words to the man are very well known.

> ...silver and gold I do not have, but what I do have I give you; In the name of Jesus Christ of Nazareth, rise up and walk.
>
> (Acts 3:6)

Peter did not pray for God to reach down his mighty hand and heal the lame man. He did not ask God to somehow send healing to the man. As a matter of fact, Peter did not pray at all! Peter knew that the Bread of Life had already been broken and was *in his hands*. This situation was really no different than the feeding of the five thousand: just distribute what has been placed in your hand! So there is only one thing to do in a situation like this: tell the lame man to get up and walk, and if he will connect with those authoritative words and act on them, the kingdom will come to his life and the miracle will occur. We must know our position of authority in Christ and speak accordingly.

What will happen if we do not boldly declare the will of God into the natural arena? The enemy will score another win! He is constantly declaring his intentions, and his declaration will stand, unless we overrule it! Remember the story of David and Goliath? The Philistine giant said to David, in 1 Samuel 17:44, "Come to me, and I will give your flesh to the birds of the air and the beasts of the field!" David was not daunted by this, but as the covenantal representative of Almighty God, he issued his decree.

> Then David said to the Philistine, "You come to me with a sword, with a spear, and with a javelin. But I come to you in the name of the Lord of hosts, the God of the armies of Israel, whom you have defied. This day the Lord will deliver you into my hand, and I will strike you and take your head from you. And this day I will give the carcasses of the camp of the Philistines to the birds of the air and the wild beasts of the earth, that all the earth may know that there is a God in Israel."
>
> (1Samuel 17: 45, 46)

The words of Goliath would have stood, had David refrained from declaring the will of God! But before that day was finished, David had struck Goliath and taken his head from his shoulders, just as he had spoken. Never be intimidated by the threats of the enemy! His is not the voice of authority. He does not have the final word. Overturn the decision of the devil with the word of the Living God! Make no exceptions! Do not be passive! Declare the will of God with confidence!

The Bible says,

> "...I am God, and there is none like Me, declaring the end from the beginning, and from ancient times things that are not yet done, saying, 'My counsel shall stand, and I will do all my pleasure'..."
>
> (Isaiah 46: 9b, 10)

God stands at the beginning of his plan, and declares the final result. And if we are to walk in true dominion, we will, like our Father, declare the end from the beginning. We must always be careful, however, to speak the final outcome, *not the process!* It is not our job to advise God, in regard to strategy! You may have heard someone request agreement in prayer for something like this: "Please pray with me that God will move my daughter and son-in-law to Seattle, and give him a job at Microsoft, and give them Christian neighbors to encourage them, and cause them to attend that large church on the west side with that dynamic pastor…"

Anyone who prays, or makes a declaration like this, is completely out of line! No one gave us authority to sit in our easy chair, devise a master plan, and then send God to carry it out! God Almighty is not our errand boy! *He* sits on the throne! *He* makes the plans! We are, however, on stable ground when we ask the Lord of the harvest, to send laborers into the fields of our loved ones. We can certainly pray in faith for the blessing and spiritual growth of our family members, because this is the *desired end*; but it is entirely up to God to devise the plan that brings it all about. Let's not waste valuable time praying our detailed plan. It probably wasn't God's will anyway. Search the Word for his intended purpose, declare it boldly, and we will see things begin to change. God produced all of creation with words. We will recreate it with words.

Let our prayer be filled with thanksgiving and worship, let our minds be filled with God's wisdom, and let our words be filled with kingdom authority.

A Kingdom of Strategy

There is nothing haphazard about God. He declares his intent and purpose long before a visible manifestation occurs. He sees the end from the beginning, the finished work from the start. Everything exists and operates according to the divine plan. From the microscopic to the astronomical, every detail is strategically in place.

Mankind—perhaps motivated by a juvenile attempt to divest himself of responsibility, or perhaps simply unwilling to accept a complexity that cannot be contained in the human mind—has settled on a lame philosophy of randomness to somehow explain the origin and development of life, while every particle of the universe screams out, "Design!" No one is as blind as the one who refuses to see.

But God is not influenced at all by any of this. He, in his omniscience, saw the futile thinking that would inevitably be produced by a godless mind, and warned us over and over not to forget that everything finds its beginning in him.

God is a planner, builder, designer, developer, and finisher. And the overpowering beauty and intelligence of God's plans have inexplicably amazed the one who caught even the smallest glimpse.

Humankind, created in God's likeness, was endowed with an incalculable ability to reason and strategize, but through the open door of sin, stupidity entered, and the human IQ was reduced exponentially. This diminished ability to understand is in one way a blessing of mercy, for otherwise, man could have invented a way to destroy himself almost immediately.

Planning Is Proactive

Since the beginning, God never intended for mankind to live in a reactionary fashion, and God, in his redemptive purchase, made provision for man to live in the wisdom of Christ. God wants his people to live wisely, in a strategic manner.

The devil however, has spent much of his existence trying to thwart the plan of God, when he really didn't know what the plan was exactly. And because he cannot predict God's next move, he finds himself reacting to it—a day late and a dollar short. But this is not always the case when Satan deals with people; we have been trained to believe that life is what it is, and we are just along for the ride. This sets us up for reactionary living and situational exploitation by the enemy.

What if we could move proactively through life? What if we could decide some things in our future rather than just being whacked by life, and then wondering what to do about it? I am not insinuating that there is an *absolute* lack of planning in the lives of most people. I am encouraged when I see families with sound spiritual, educational, and financial plans. But there are many things that we unquestionably accept as our 'lot in life', that perhaps could have been avoided by proactive measures. I am not suggesting that all difficulties are avoidable. As a matter of fact, the Bible guarantees us that we will have problems. But how much of it is life, and how much is the result of our enemy's battle plan against us?

Let's look at it in its simplest terms. God has a plan for each individual life within the mosaic of his grand scheme. That plan is composed of all the good thoughts that God thinks with regard to his children—thoughts to prosper, protect, and bless. That plan needs to find its way into our imagination and be formed into words, so that our mouth can plant them as seeds into our future. Many of the events that we encounter today are fruit from seeds we planted yesterday.

The enemy also has a plan for us. His plan includes disease, ruin, and death, but that plan must also find its way into our mind and mouth in order to become a reality. Here is where authoritative speaking comes strongly into play. I firmly believe that God's plan for my life does not include Alzheimer's disease, diabetes, disaster, untimely death, or any such thing. So I have a wonderful opportunity to stand each morning *before* life happens to me and declare victory, safety, prosperity, and health into my life and the lives of those under my influence. I have adopted the plan of God as my own, and I will speak that *only* into my future. I have read the Scriptures from cover to cover, and nowhere is it found that sickness and degeneration is something I should accept. The Bible does say, however, that the law of the Spirit of life in Christ Jesus has freed me from the law of sin and death (Romans 8: 2). So I declare *that* truth into my future, knowing that sickness and degeneration cannot just 'happen' in my family. The word of God *happened* to the devil and broke the arrow in his bow before he could release it. That is proactive living.

Planning Leads to Success

I am saddened as I watch some of my friends and relatives live from crisis to crisis. Their lives are not ordered according to a plan; crisis holds the position of authority in their lives. Crises determine their next move, and because there is not a visible leader in the home, they just drift through life with a continual bumping into crisis. Many times, they are not encountering a new crisis, but rather an old familiar one. The saying "If you do what you've always done, you will get what you've always got," is still true. When one bad situation is finally resolved, a common thinking person will relax as if all is well forevermore and fail to anticipate the next situation. I am convinced that it is the space between crises that can be used to determine how soon you will have another. A successful life is one that is ordered according to a plan. Some within our modern society would contend that planning is more of a personality issue. Those who enjoy making plans should do it, and those who are not so inclined should not be burdened with it. But if this were true, then failure and success would also be considered personality issues.

The Bible instructs us to bear the fruit of the Spirit, which are love, joy, peace, patience, kindness, goodness, faithfulness, gentleness, and self-control. There are no disclaimers or exemption clauses. We are *all* to cultivate these characteristics in our lives regardless of personality. These are the characteristics of truly successful people, and they are not developed accidentally. Noble-minded people intentionally develop winning traits in their lives despite status or situation, pedigree, or personality. If you plan on having a good successful life, you must successfully work your good plan.

Emotional versus Intellectual

Dave Ramsey said, "Children do what feels good; adults devise a plan and follow it." The concept of planning is what separates children from adults. The difference between maturity and immaturity is planning. The difference between responsibility and irresponsibility is planning. The difference between those who will live eternally with Christ and those who will not, is *planning*.

Jesus communicated this truth to us by way of a short story.

> Then the kingdom of heaven will be like ten bridesmaids who took their lamps and went to meet the bridegroom. Five of them were foolish, and five were wise. The five who were foolish didn't take enough olive oil for their lamps, but the other five were wise enough to take along extra oil. When the bridegroom was delayed, they all became drowsy and fell asleep. At midnight they were roused by the shout, "Look,

the bridegroom is coming! Come out and meet him!" All the bridesmaids got up and prepared their lamps. Then the five foolish ones asked the others, "Please give us some of your oil because our lamps are going out." But the others replied, "We don't have enough for all of us. Go to a shop and buy some for yourselves." But while they were gone to buy oil, the bridegroom came. Then *those who were ready* went in with him to the marriage feast, and the door was locked. Later, when the other five bridesmaids returned, they stood outside, calling, "Lord! Lord! Open the door for us!" But he called back, "Believe me, I don't know you!"

Matthew 25:1–12 (NLT, emphasis mine)

Jesus is preparing a place for us, and he plans to spend eternity with those who have been preparing themselves for him. The level of importance that we ascribe to something in our lives will determine the amount of preparation invested into it.

The difference between the wise and foolish bridesmaids was the level of their preparedness.

It was not as though the foolish ones were *completely* unprepared. After all, they did have oil in their lamps. But a certain amount of emotional complacency had kept them from having *enough* oil. Making a plan and getting prepared based upon an emotional assessment of the situation is seldom a good idea. Emotions are good. God created them, and they have a place in our lives just as reasoning does, but few people recognize the level of influence that emotions have in their decision making.

Let's look for a moment at the differences between emotion and intellect without vilifying either one.

The human soul consists of three parts:

1. The will– Decision-making faculty.
2. The mind– Reasoning, calculating faculty.
3. The emotions,– Internal senses and ability to feel.

I like to illustrate the human soul by drawing an equilateral acute triangle and writing *will* at the apex, then writing *mind* and *emotions* at the two lower corners. The human will stands at the head and is the ruling authority over the entire being. Its function is to draw data from both the mind and emotions, and then make an intelligent decision. The difficulty with this is that the emotions have a louder voice than the mind, in many cases. Emotions are predominantly self-concerned with their greatest efforts aimed at preserving *the feeling* of inward security. Emotions can advise the mind and the will of inward pain and trauma, but because the emotional department has no ability to process facts or truth, it consequently has no ability to implement wholesome productive countermeasures. The emotions, in a noble attempt to preserve the feeling of internal security, will often settle on a "solution" that leads to a future problem of greater consequence, but that is not a concern if the immediate feeling of security is restored.

The mind processes data gathered from the five physical senses and is primarily concerned with cause and effect. The mind has no ability to effectively process subjective matter, such as feelings, no more than a thermometer can measure wind speed. It is not designed to do so; that is the function of the emotions. The mind draws most of its data from the outside; emotions are concerned with what is happening on the inside. Both the mind and the emotions have the ability to store data in the form of retrievable memory. The emotions file information in the form of sensation while the mind stores data in the form of thought, containing words and pictures. The emotional faculty has no long-term vision; it is completely absorbed in the status of the present moment. The mind is largely occupied with finding a reasonable conclusion by weighing options, comparing data with data, and running historical analyses to see how things were done in the past. The function of the mind is to present clear objective reasoning to the will. The function of the emotions is to advise the will in the area of subjectivity and security. The will must be strong enough to make a reasonable decision in spite of any selfish influence from the emotions. The will must be able to say to the emotions, "I understand your sense of insecurity and fear. I am currently drawing information from the mind, and will make the best possible decision to solve the problem, without causing a greater one in the process."

An untrained set of emotions will kick and scream initially, but ironically enough, will learn to appreciate the greater security that comes from sound decision making. The emotions make a wonderful traveling companion, if they trust the decisions of the mind and will.

I heard Joseph Garlington once said, "We make emotional decisions, then use reasoning to justify them."

Consider this scenario: A person, who is struggling financially, makes plans to balance their checkbook and start a budget. But after coming home from a hard day's work, the emotions begin to speak. "I am exhausted. I'll do this tomorrow. I don't feel like doing this right now." Now if the will is actually in charge of this person, it will allow the mind to speak also. "Yes, I am tired, but *not* exhausted. (*Exhausted* means "*entirely* used up, *completely* drained, spent." The emotions tend to use superlatives to dramatize their argument: "you *never*, you *always*, I'm *exhausted*, etc.") I do have a little strength left. If I balance the checkbook now, I will be one step closer to financial order. If I put it off until tomorrow, I probably won't feel like doing it then either, and "putting it off until tomorrow" is precisely why we're in this mess today! The will then weighs the information and says, "If I cave in to the way I feel, my situation will never change, so I will balance my checkbook now, and then rest." Later that night, the emotions speak again, "Wow, it sure feels good to have that checkbook balanced!"

Now, before you laugh off this somewhat facetious illustration, let us remember that the thoughts passing through our minds may have originated in the emotional arena. Many people are not aware of the fact that there are two completely different compartments within us, each one producing thought—the mind, which is concerned with logic and rationale, and the emotions, which are mainly interested in self-gratification.

I am not suggesting that resisting selfish impulse is always easy when the loudest voice in our psyche is voting for short-term pleasure and long term grief, but it must be done in order to live proactively.

The actions of the foolish bridesmaids speak clearly, "I am excited about meeting the bridegroom, but I hope he comes early, because my lamp doesn't hold enough oil to last until midnight, and I really don't want to carry around an extra container. What a hassle! He'll probably come before long, I'll be okay."

Conversely, the actions of the wise also speak, "This is one wedding I cannot afford to miss! My lamp is full of oil, and I brought my wick trimmer and an extra container with enough oil to last until midnight if necessary. I have planned for this event, and I am ready!"

Carrying an extra container was most likely an inconvenience, but it spoke loudly to the groom that he was worth every possible measure of preparation. It is my personal belief that Christ will wait until the "midnight hour" in order to test the wisdom and determination of his followers. Those who have not planned to marry the king probably won't. Some are preparing to be everything that he wants in a bride, while others have been infatuated only with their own salvation.

Do You Have a Plan?

It has been said that most people do not plan to fail; they just fail to plan. If your life were illustrated by a pie graph, how many segments would be ordered according to a plan and how many are allowed to play out haphazardly? God has placed every person in a managerial position. We are called to manage the life that he loaned to us. Another word for *manager* is *steward*. The word translated *manager* or *steward* in the Bible is *oikonomos*, which literally means "to arrange the house." Our English word *economy* is a derivative; thus, an economy, whether in a household or in a nation is the "arrangement of the house." As managers of our own lives and households, we have the unshakeable responsibility of arranging the house according to a well thought out plan. Economies operate, by and large, the way they were designed to operate. They are stable if they were designed to be stable. They rise and fall if they were originally designed to rise and fall. They are a creation and reflection of the manager's ideals, and function according to a plan; they do not have a mind of their own. The spiritual, financial, and relational condition of our homes is not the outcome of some cosmic roll-of-the-dice, but a direct result of our planning, or lack thereof.

Our lives and the lives of those under our influence have been lent to us by the Lord, and his delight will be to say to us, "Well done good and faithful servant; you were faithful over a few things, I will make you ruler over many things. Enter into the joy of your Lord." (Matthew 25: 21, NKJV).

God is looking for planners, faithful managers, who proactively decide on the atmosphere of their home. We must do as Joshua did and declare openly and intentionally that we and those with us will serve the Lord. Followers are many, good leaders are few; let's devise a Godly plan and then live it out.

People With a Plan

The story of Joseph serves as a wonderful illustration of planning. Almost a decade and a half before it was "time," God's plan to save that part of the world through Joseph was already in motion. He capitalized on Satan's malicious scheme to destroy Joseph, and used it for the transportation part of his own plan.

Not everything went well for Joseph in Egypt. He was sold as a slave, and after his master's wife tried unsuccessfully to seduce him, she lied about him, and he ended up in prison. But Joseph obviously had a plan for his own life, a plan to maintain his integrity before God, even in the face of temptation and imprisonment; a plan to honor God and allow his will to be done.

It is approximately thirteen years after his arrival in Egypt that we find Joseph, due to some very unique events, standing before the Pharaoh and declaring the interpretation to the king's disturbing dreams. Before the sun set that evening, Joseph's entire life changed, and he stepped into his purpose and destiny. No more a prisoner, he was now the second most powerful man in the largest empire. This had happened not because Joseph interpreted Pharaoh's dreams, but because he had a plan!

When Joseph had finished interpreting the dreams, he presented his own advice and simply laid out before Pharaoh a strategy for preparation that included specific numbers and percentages. I am sure that Joseph was not overly concerned with the presumptuousness of his actions, after all, he had come from prison, and he had nothing to lose. But the Pharaoh was an astute leader, however, and recognized the wisdom of God in Joseph's life and logically concluded that there was no one better qualified to oversee such an important project.

"So the advice was good in the eyes of Pharaoh and in the eyes of all his servants" (Genesis 41: 37, NKJV).

Pharaoh was impressed with Joseph's God after the dreams were interpreted, but he was impressed with Joseph after a practical plan had been laid out. Ultimately, it was God's plan of salvation that came to pass.

When God gave Noah the task of building the ark, He also gave him a detailed plan.

> Make yourself an ark of gopherwood; make rooms in the ark, and cover it inside and outside with pitch. And this is how you shall make it: The length shall be 300 cubits [approx. 450 feet], its width 50 cubits [approx. 75 feet], and its height 30 cubits [approx. 45 feet].
>
> Genesis 6: 14, 15 (NKJV, brackets mine)

God was very specific about his dimensions and details. Ship builders, for centuries, scorned the design of the ark, saying it was too long and narrow. It was close to the dawn of the nineteenth century before engineers discovered that the symmetry of the ark is the most stable in turbulent waters.

Moses received an incredibly detailed plan for the tabernacle of meeting, and everything related to it—from the ball-and-socket design of its joints to the moldings and relief work in hammered gold. Moses was not merely *instructed* by God, but was also allowed to gaze into heaven itself and *see* for the purpose of small-scale duplication, *the temple of God and all its furnishings*! He saw the *real* ark of the covenant with living cherubim covering the mercy seat, the lampstand with seven branches illuminated by the seven Spirits of God, the showbread (literally the "bread of presence") upon its table of gold. Moses looked into heaven while God gave him details and measurements for the model that would stand in the center of Israeli life for centuries. It did not take forty days and nights to receive the Ten Commandments; it took *eighty* days and nights to receive the commandments and all of the details and measurements of the tabernacle, with one small interruption in the middle to handle an idolatrous uprising.

"And see to it that you make them according to the pattern which was *shown* you on the mountain" (Exodus 25:40, NKJV, emphasis mine).

The magnificent temple of Solomon was actually built from detailed plans given to King David by the Holy Spirit.

> Then David gave his son Solomon the *plans* for the vestibule, its houses, its treasuries, its upper chambers, its inner chambers, and the place of the mercy seat; and the plans for all that he had *by the Spirit*, of the courts of the house of the Lord, of all the chambers all around, of the treasuries of the house of God, and of the treasuries for the dedicated things… All this," said David, *"The Lord made me understand in writing, by His hand upon me, all the works of these plans."*
>
> 1 Chronicles 28:11, 12, 19 (NKJV, emphasis mine)

Perhaps the most expensive temple to ever rest upon this planet was God's own design! Scripture is filled with detailed plans that emanate from the mind of God. There is nothing random about God; nothing is left to chance. The entire universe shouts out the immeasurable brilliance of his design, and beyond any doubt, the most stunning of all is the plan to redeem his children and reinstate them in his kingdom.

> Then the King will say to those on His right hand, "Come, you blessed of My Father, inherit the kingdom *prepared for you from the foundation of the world.*"
>
> Matthew 25:34 (NKJV, emphasis mine)

> Just as He chose us in Him *before the foundation of the world*, that we should be holy and without blame before Him in love.
>
> Ephesians 1:4 (NKJV, emphasis mine)

God is a designer and planner; and those who follow him are filled with his will, purpose, and design.

Training the Children

God is not haphazard in any part of his work, including the training of his children. When it comes to developing his sons and daughters, he has a definite plan. God has given many instructions in his word concerning parenting and child discipline, and it never ceases to amaze me, how seemingly wise people will dismiss the Biblical directives in lieu of some new modern philosophy, and actually expect it to work. God understands the dynamics of the human soul more than anyone; he created it, so there is no "better" way of doing it. One good look at modern society should convince anyone that the way children are brought up in this nation as a whole, is simply not working.

Many children are raised; fewer are trained. Raising offspring is relatively easy; you give them food and a little water, and they grow. Training a child, however, requires so much more. Training is that intentional, methodical, consistent shaping of a child's value system and logic process that causes them to have a reverence for God and a respect for their fellow man. One of the most common, and perhaps the most dangerous mistakes that parents can make, is allowing their child to make their own decisions before they are ready. In our culture today, there seems to be more said about respecting a youngster's right to make their own decisions than there is about training them to make the right ones. Nowhere else in society is this philosophy accepted. If a young man or woman joins the military, they are told what to wear, when to get up in the morning, how to act, what to think, and what to do all day long. If they opt for a more specialized field, the training only intensifies. The military must dismantle the old paradigm of individuality and the old habits of behavior in order to create a good soldier. Some officers speak of, "Getting into their heads, and telling them what to think." The irony is this: people accept the military strategy as a completely normal way of training, and applaud the disciplined leaders that it produces, but strongly oppose the idea of implementing anything like it in the home. The method of training in some households, is merely allowing the child to "learn from their own mistakes." While this is a valuable tool if used strategically, some parents have relied upon it almost exclusively, thus, effectively abdicating their mentorship role. There is usually one right way to do something surrounded by a thousand wrong ways, and if a parent sits back and allows their children to explore all the wrong paths and just trusts that eventually they will somehow land on the right one, their child can only conclude that their parents were selfish and did not care enough to steer them toward success. The logical breakdown of this philosophy is that people do *not* learn from fatal mistakes; it is simply the end of their road. What kind of teacher would use this as their training method? The Bible calls this hatred.

"Train up a child in the way he should go, and when he is old he will not depart from it" (Proverbs 22: 6, NKJV). This verse contains a vitally important message: train your children in the way they *should* go. Don't let them waste their formative years learning what *not to do* in life because when they are old, they will not depart from the training of their youth, even if it was wrong.

An excited young couple drives over to the construction site of their new home on the day that the concrete foundation is being poured. They do not see any forms or stakes or strings, just an empty lot. The contractor explains that since foundations are so important to the building, it is best to let the concrete decide which way it wants to go. The cement truck arrives, the concrete is poured out into a big pile, and the truck leaves. The contractor explains to the horrified couple that there really is no point in making forms, because sometimes, the concrete gets out anyway, and therefore, should be allowed to express its own creativity.

How do we describe a hard, pile of concrete on a building site? Wasted and useless.

All the forms must be in place with sufficient bracing to withstand the pressure. There will be a certain window of time to shape and smooth the concrete before it is permanently set. When it is cured, the forms can be removed and the product will be exactly what you allowed it to be. So it is with our children.

Simply put, people do what people are trained to do. Parents who use the ancient worn-out excuse, "Why tell them what to do; they're just going to rebel and do their own thing anyway," are perpetuating an untrained society. Train your child that sexual immorality is wrong and will lead to heartache as well as judgment. By doing so, you will build a spiritual and psychological "fence" in their lives, and even if they rebel and cross over the line, they will always know where the fence is, and on which side they are. Their heart knows where moral "home" is, and when they are older, the training of their parents calls them to return.

Many parents today have a "what's the use" mentality and don't bother creating that moral "fence" in their children's soul, resulting in confused, angry people that are unsure of the fine points of right and wrong because they were raised, but not trained.

One of the reasons that God chose Abraham as his covenant partner was the fact that Abraham would be diligent to train his offspring in the way of the Lord.

> For I have known him, in order that he may *command his children* and his household after him, that they keep the way of the Lord, to do righteousness and justice, that the Lord may bring to Abraham what He has spoken to him.
>
> Genesis 18: 19 (NKJV, emphasis mine)

The effectiveness of this covenant rested on Abraham's faithfulness to train his children in it!

Don't let society tell you that you shouldn't command your children. There is a mixed-up world out there ready to jump at the chance to train your child, should you relax in your efforts.

The next generation belongs to the one who trains them.

Calling Them Out

In the movie *Courageous*, Alex Kendrick admonishes father's to "call out the man" in their sons. This is one of the most powerful things a man can do! Fathers and mothers, it is time for a godly parenting plan! Speak to the man or woman that is being developed inside your child. Tell them how to think, what to value, what to believe, and how to behave. No one else on the planet has more influence in their lives than you.

Fathers, teach him how to lead, how to be strong of character, how to have courage, and how to communicate. Cultivate a confidence in who he is becoming in Christ that will cause him to stand when everyone around is sitting, to cry even when others are watching, and to do the right thing when no one seems to notice. Develop within him the valor to protect those under his care, the nobility to take responsibility for his words, attitudes, and actions, the tenderness to nurture, and the vulnerability to love. Only a father can teach these things.

Mothers, teach your daughters how to be discreet, how to live unselfishly, how to be nurturing, kind, and gentle. Cultivate a confidence in who she is becoming in Christ that will cause her to understand her value, and keep her from selling it cheaply; keep her from the pitfall of vain competition and from feeling threatened or diminished by the thought of submission to her future husband. Develop within her the inward beauty of a meek and gentle spirit, the elegance of social grace, the attractiveness of self-discipline, and the necessity of selflessness.

When these traits are molded within your child and they have come of age, it is the beautiful responsibility of the parents to declare to them their adulthood.

The Jewish Bar-Mitzvah stands as a division between childhood and manhood. It is deliberate and decisive. Yesterday, you were a child; today, you are a man. In Orthodox Judaism, there is no confusing stage of adolescence where they are no longer a child, but not yet an adult. This is a man-made social problem. Young people grope through this time, unsure of who they are and what is expected of them. Their emotions do not want to lose the lighter responsibilities of childhood, but struggle to break into the freedoms of maturity. So being neither child nor adult, the uncertainty continues until someone draws a line and says, "This is the point of adulthood."

It is not the decision of an ungodly government to suggest that childhood is officially over at age twenty-one, but rather, godly parents who call out the man or woman in their sons and daughters.

God's Ultimate Plan for You

The Bible declares that Jesus is planning to present us to his Father, faultless and perfect (Jude 24). This, of course, is totally contingent upon our cooperation with him. Our transformation is a joint effort.

Christianity calls out to the world, "God accepts you just the way you are!", and while this is certainly true, there remains a subtle inclination to believe that God is *completely happy* with you the way you are. This is certainly *not* true. It has never been a secret that he fully intends to totally transform us into his own image of perfection. We may come to him the way we are, but he is certainly not going to allow us to stay that way! We must humble ourselves and realize that we are a project, not a masterpiece, and as we allow him to work his plan in our lives, we are the better for it. Many times, people accept Christ as Savior and allow him to forgive their sin and place them into the kingdom of God, but somehow expect to retain their old logic, priority, and value systems. Some try to "merge" with Christianity and create a coexistence where God has a place in their lives, but they are allowed to maintain their own identity.

God did not come into our lives to give us a simple tune up and a five-point inspection, then, call us good and send us down the road. He fully intends to perform a complete restoration where every piece is removed and every piece is fixed or changed. Every single part of us must be submitted to him, even the ones that seem to be in perfect working order. We tend to think in compartmentalized fashion when it comes to Christianity. We offer God only our spirit because that is where the sin is contained, not realizing that sin crept through every part of us like yeast in bread dough. God is not content to have a part of us; he needs *all* of us in order to do his perfect work. The more we hold back, the longer it takes. The more we resist, the more we sabotage our own lives. The sooner we surrender, the sooner we are transformed. Perfection is God's ultimate plan for you.

Faith:
The Kingdom Connection

Kingdom faith, as described in the Scriptures, is very simple and easy to understand. The complicated philosophies and opinions that have sprung up around it are all man-made. Faith in its purest form is inherent in the smallest child. It is usually the experienced adult who struggles most in the area of faith.

Demystifying Faith

Faith is not an abstract force. The Scriptures declare that faith is tangible, something far more prevailing than a wish. It is substance and evidence of unseen things.

"Now faith is the substance of things hoped for, the evidence of things not seen" (Hebrews 11:1, NKJV).

Faith is not mere mental assent. It is a firm persuasion that is rooted deep in the heart and is evidenced by the action that one takes; therefore, faith is exhibited not only in the words we speak, but also in the decisions we make.

Faith has strength and ability. Faith has power. Faith is *the connection* to the kingdom of God. Faith is our spiritual arm and hand used for grasping things in the spiritual realm and bringing them into the natural arena. It is our spiritual grip. When a person has taken hold of something in the supernatural world, they know that they have it long before anyone else does. They have reached into God's grace with their hand of faith and wrapped their fingers around the answer and are completely assured of it. There is a certain tangibility to this connection with grace. The one exercising their faith can "feel" the substance in their spiritual hand.

Don't Lose Your Grip

As I stated in a previous chapter, the apostle Paul used an olive tree metaphor to illustrate that anyone, at any time, can be attached to the covenant of God through faith; and anyone, at any time, can be disconnected from it through unbelief. Faith is the connection.

The covenant of God is unshakeable; it can never move. Our connection to it is the only factor in the equation that is variable. We decide if we are going to attach ourselves to the covenant of God, and we decide if we are going to disconnect.

A person who rappels down the side of a mountain is not as concerned with how strong and secure the mountain is, as he is with the integrity of his gear and the reliability of the attachment point. If he falls, it will not be because the mountain was not strong enough to hold him, but because his attachment to it was not secure. God has provided, not only the priceless gift of grace, but also the gear needed to connect us to it—the faith of God.

Scripture warns us over and over, not to allow our faith to weaken, or we will lose our grip on the covenant of God.

> Moreover, brethren, I declare to you the gospel which I preached to you, which also you received and in which you stand, by which also you are saved, *if you hold fast* that word which I preached to you—unless you believed in vain.
>
> 1 Corinthians 15:1, 2 (NKJV, emphasis mine)

Paul says that you are saved *if* you don't let go. Don't lose your grip.

> And you, who once were alienated and enemies in your mind by wicked works, yet now He has reconciled in the body of His flesh through death, to present you holy, and blameless, and above reproach in His sight—*if indeed you continue in the faith*, grounded and steadfast, and *are not moved away* from the hope of the gospel which you heard, which was preached to every creature under heaven, of which I, Paul, became a minister.
>
> Colossians 1:21–23 (NKJV, emphasis mine)

Again, the Apostle Paul declares the redemptive work of Christ Jesus, and his plan to present us blameless and holy before God, reminding us that this is completely contingent upon our remaining connected through faith. Don't lose your grip.

> And Moses indeed was faithful in all his house as a servant, for a testimony of those things

> which would be spoken afterward, but Christ as
> a Son over His own house, whose house we are
> *if we hold fast* the confidence and the rejoicing
> of the hope firm to the end.
>
> Hebrews 3:5, 6 (NKJV, emphasis mine)

The writer of Hebrews clearly shows us that Christ's house is composed of those people who hold fast, firm to the end. Don't lose your grip!

> For we have become partakers of Christ, *if we*
> *hold the beginning of our confidence steadfast to the*
> *end.*
>
> Hebrews 3;14 (NKJV, emphasis mine)

The race is won not because you started strong, but because you finished strong! The partakers of Christ are seen here as those who held on all the way to the end. How do we hold on? By our faith. How do we disconnect from Christ. By losing our grip and letting go of the kingdom of God. Don't lose your grip!

The apostle Paul in 1Corinthians 15:1, 2, is not speaking to unsaved people, he is addressing those who had *received* the gospel who were *standing* in the gospel and who were *saved*; then, he reminds them that all of this is true, unless of course, they let go of it. Paul, again in Colossians 1:21–23, is speaking to those *who have been reconciled*; not unbelievers.

There are many other scriptures that point, not only at the wonderful grace of God, but also at our connection to it. Here are just a few:

- That Christ may dwell in your hearts *through faith* (Ephesians 3:17).
- Therefore *do not cast away your confidence,* which has great reward (Hebrews 10:35).
- Now the just shall live by faith, but if anyone *draws back* (Hebrews 10:38).
- But we are not of those who *draw back* (Hebrews 10:39).
- Who are *kept* by the power of God *through faith* (1 Peter 1:3–5).
- Better for them not to have known the way of righteousness, than having known it, *to turn* (2 Peter 2:21).
- Beware lest you *fall from your own steadfastness* (2 Peter 3:17).

The message of scripture is overwhelming. *Don't lose your grip on grace!*

The Importance of Faith

> But without faith, it is impossible to please Him, for he who comes to God must believe that He is, and that He is a rewarder of those who diligently seek Him.
>
> Hebrews 11:6 (NKJV)

This verse clearly tells us that it is not within the realm of possibility to please God, without faith. Or we could say it this way, "God is pleased with those who have faith in his word!" In Romans 14:23, we are told that whatever is not of faith, is sin.

Why is faith so important to God? The answer is simple: there is no other way to be connected to his kingdom. Why is God so displeased with faithlessness? Because there is nothing more insulting than to act as if his word to us is unsound. People with great faith are the ones commended by God. They are so sure that God's power is not only great, but also available to them, and they connect to it with an iron grip of faith and simply refuse to let go! God is greatly pleased with them because they prove with their actions that his promises are unbreakable.

Faith is the only way to access covenant.

In the days of Jesus's earthly ministry, the Jews had their own version of eternal security. They believed that they were inseparable from the covenant because they were the blood descendants of Abraham. Jesus told them plainly that physical pedigree meant nothing. Abraham connected to God's covenant through faith; therefore, all who will ever be connected to it will do so through faith. Just as God's word created, and still yet maintains, the existence of the universe, so our faith creates the connection to the covenant grace of God and continually maintains that connection. As long as our faith remains, the connection remains. We *are* eternally secure *if we hold fast our confidence firm to the end*. Nowhere do the Scriptures teach that we are secure in grace, *apart from faith*. Faith is the attachment point.

There is more said in the New Testament about faith than about grace, which is perfectly logical, because the gift of grace is the *constant* in God's equation; it is our faith which is the only variable. The deciding factor is not God's power, but our faith.

Where Does Faith Come From?

There are only three passages of Scripture that tell us how faith comes to be, in the hearts of people.

- For I say through the grace given to me, to everyone who is among you, not to think of himself more highly than he ought to think, but to think soberly, as God has dealt to each one a measure of faith (Romans 12:3, NKJV).
- Consequently, faith *comes from listening, and listening comes through the Word of God* (Romans 10:17, ISV, emphasis mine).
- Looking unto *Jesus, the author* and finisher of our faith (Hebrews 12:2a, NKJV, emphasis mine).

Faith comes from God and his word placed in the hearts of people. But like all of God's gifts, it is deposited in the form of a seed, and it is up to us to cultivate it and cause it to grow. God knows that sinners cannot connect with the gospel message without faith, so the seed of faith is germinated within them by the hearing of the word! Then, as the word is given more influence in their lives, faith begins to thrive.

> Then His disciples came to Him and awoke Him, saying, "Lord, save us! We are perishing!" but He said to them, "Why are you fearful, O you of *little faith*?" Then He arose and rebuked the winds and the sea, and there was a great calm.
>
> Matthew 8:25, 26 (NKJV, emphasis mine)

Jesus is not given to sarcasm, nor is he unreasonable. He was not poking fun at these men because they were afraid. Jesus was pointing out that there was *no reason* to be fearful.

But what about the storm? Can a storm defeat the Word of God? Of course not!

The disciples were fearful because they had *underdeveloped* faith. The Greek word translated "little faith" in this verse is *oligopistis*, which literally means "underdeveloped faith." When God puts within every human being a measure of faith, he fully intends that we exercise it, stretch it, and strengthen it by reason of use. God invests kingdom substance into us, and he expects a healthy return on his investment. When God gives us a seed, he is expecting that we ultimately present him with a fruit-bearing tree grown from that seed. When he lends five talents, he anticipates ten in return. In our covenant partnership with God, he puts up the capital, and we put up the stewardship. He invests the seed; we invest a little work. This is why Jesus chided his disciples for their underdeveloped faith. Their faith should have been stronger than it was. They had been irresponsible with God's investment of faith in their lives.

Should we pray and ask God to increase our faith? The disciples did in Luke 17:5, "And the apostles said to the Lord, 'Increase our faith.' So the Lord said, 'If you have faith as a mustard seed, you can say to this mulberry tree, "Be pulled up by the roots and be planted in the sea," and it would obey you.'"

Jesus did not agree to increase their faith, but he did bring them back to the realization that the small seed of faith that God initially invested in them was enough to uproot a mulberry tree and transplant it in the ocean. It is not God's job to increase our faith; it is ours. He planted the seed; we cultivate and fertilize it.

As I stated in a previous chapter, the wrong question to ask is "How much faith is enough?" The amount of faith you have is enough to move mountains—if you fuel it with patience, and don't smother it with the facts.

I've seen many people, in the midst of crises, trying to build their faith. Don't focus on faith, focus on the word, and faith will naturally grow. Faith is a by-product, so to speak, of meditating on the infallible covenant of God Almighty. The Holy Spirit has come to guide us into all truth, testify to Christ, and remind us of all that he said. In essence, the Holy Spirit came to solidify our place in Christ. If we are completely saturated with the word of God, bearing the fruit of faith is inevitable.

Faith does not come through the laying on of hands, so don't let someone try to *impart* faith into you. It may sound like a good idea, but it is not based on the Scriptures, so it simply will not work.

Now This Is Faith!

Once when Jesus was passing through a particular village, a woman with an incurable flow of blood pressed through the crowd and finally managed to get close enough to him to touch the border of his cloak. She had said within herself, "If only I may touch his garment, I shall be made well." Jesus stopped and said, "Who touched me?" The disciples were amazed at his question because they were continuously jostled by the crowd around them. But this touch was different. Jesus had felt power *leave* his body and knew that someone had touched him with *faith*. The frightened woman was brought before Jesus, "And He said to her, 'Daughter, be of good cheer; your faith has made you well. Go in peace'" (Luke 9:48, NKJV).

Many things can be learned from this amazing story! First of all, we can see that this woman had declared not only the end result, but also the actual connection point! Secondly, it is clear that the *function* of faith is to draw things from the supernatural realm and bring them into our situation.

This woman had simply appropriated God's power for her need. Jesus *felt* the power leave his body. Of all the physical contact that Jesus had with the thronging people, only one touch resulted in a miracle. Jesus then said to the restored woman, "Your *faith* has made you well." Religious people still struggle with these words, because after all, it was really His *power* that healed her body; faith can't actually heal anyone, right?

People don't get healed because God has the power to do so; they get healed because they form a connection with that power. Static energy cannot produce an effect, only kinetic energy. And the power of God is merely potential until someone makes a connection and closes the circuit.

When Jesus shed his blood at the scourging post and later at the cross, he made available to us the riches of heaven in the form of an open provision. This means that everything we need is found in his exquisite gift of grace, and we draw from it with our grip of faith.

Religion tends to view Christ as holding grace in his arms and deciding, per request, whether or not he will meet that need. This is *not* the way God set it up. He placed his gift of grace on the table expecting us to come boldly and take what we need by faith. When it is given in the form of an open provision, the option of refusing someone no longer exists!

Some will undoubtedly argue that we should not be so presumptuous as to simply *take* what we need from God's grace, but discern his will for us by whether or not he brings it to us. This is ignorance as well as pride. The Scriptures are brimming over with the picture of faith as *our grip* on grace, and is the perfect description of his will for us. Secondly, it is extremely arrogant to treat God as our errand boy. He isn't going to *bring* us anything because he *already brought it all;* at the cross!

If the woman with the flow of blood had watched Jesus go by, she would not have been healed, even though it was his will for her to be whole. Her faith was the reason she received her miracle.

How many times did Jesus say to someone, "My power has healed you." Not once. But to several different people, he said, "Your *faith* has made you whole." Now, some religious people worry that too much emphasis is placed upon faith when it certainly seems more pious to focus on God's ability. This would be just as productive as a math teacher who focused entirely upon the constants in an algebra problem and never the variables. The net result would be: *no answer to the problem*. It takes both. Just as the constants are important to finding the variables in algebraic equations, so grace must be coupled with faith in order to reach an answer. If the power of God is preached the way it ought to be, then faith will naturally spring up in the hearts of the listeners.

Faith and Patience

Jesus told them a story showing that it was necessary for them to pray consistently and never quit. He said, "There was once a judge in some city who never gave God a thought and cared nothing for people. A widow in that city kept after him: "My rights are being violated. Protect me!" He never gave her the time of day. But after this went on and on he said to himself, 'I care nothing what God thinks, even less what people think. But because this widow won't quit badgering me, I'd better do something and see that she gets justice—otherwise I'm going to end up beaten black-and-blue by her pounding.'"Then the Master said, "Do you hear what that judge, corrupt as he is, is saying? So what makes you think God won't step in and work justice for His chosen people, who continue to cry out for help? Won't He stick up for them? I assure you, he will. He will not drag His feet. But how much of that kind of persistent faith will the Son of Man find on the earth when He returns?"

Luke 18:1–8, (The Message)

First of all, we must realize that Jesus is not *comparing* the corrupt judge with God; he is *contrasting* the two. God is *not like* the corrupt judge; you *don't* have to pester him to get something from him. That is not the message here! This short story shows us that it is possible, through persistence, to get our petition granted from an uncaring, unjust judge. So *how much more* will our God who cares for us deeply answer our prayers. Jesus said that he would answer speedily. The widow in the parable exemplified a tenacious grip of faith. Once again, Jesus is teaching us that kingdom faith must have an element of patient persistence.

Faith is your grip on grace; patience is your ability to maintain that grip until your need is satisfied. Without patience, we won't believe long enough to receive the end result of our faith. The Bible says, "For you have need of *endurance*, so that after you have done the will of God, you may receive the promise" (Hebrews 10:36, NKJV, emphasis mine).

This verse teaches us that patient endurance is often the key to receiving the promise. We, in America, suffer from a terrible lack of patience, so we tend to perceive the kingdom of God through that filter. Many, many people fail to receive their answer from God simply because they abort the mission just before it is fully accomplished. In our culture, we tend to believe God until we're tired, instead of believing God until we have the answer.

"And we desire that each one of you show the same diligence to the *full assurance of hope until the end*, that you do not become sluggish, but imitate those who through *faith and patience inherit the promises*" (Hebrews 6:11, 12, NKJV, emphasis mine).

| Robert Cochran Smith Jr. M.Th.

We need to find people in the kingdom that are living in the blessing of God, and do what they are doing! The people who receive their answer from God do not have a fancy, complicated theology; they just believe the covenant Word of God all the way to the end. They have a grip, and they won't let go! These kind of people are pleasing to God because they are beginning to show the traits of their Father. His unshakeable character is being reproduced in his children.

The Bible, speaking of Abraham, says, "And so, after he had patiently endured, he obtained the promise" (Hebrews 6:15, NKJV).

If we grasp hold of the covenant Word of promise and hold on as Abraham did, then it is *inevitable* that we receive the answer! There is no way around it. If we believe in the covenant the way Abraham did, we're going to get what Abraham got—the blessing!

The Ability to See

There is no such thing as "blind faith." A person may have a blind hope, but faith is not blind. Faith is the ability to see into the supernatural world. My mother once wrote, "To believe the impossible, one must first see the invisible." The Bible says, "While we do not look at the things which are seen, but at the things which are *not seen*. For the things which are seen are temporary, but the things which are not seen are eternal" (2 Corinthians 4:18, NKJV, emphasis mine).

This verse says that we are to look at unseen things. How is this possible? With the eyes of faith. Abraham could *see* both himself *and* his son returning from the mountain. Job failed to see the infallibility of God's word until God arrested his attention, and then he said, "I had heard of You [only] by the hearing of the ear, *but now my [spiritual] eye sees You*" (Job 42:5, Amplified Bible, emphasis mine).

Great leaders are said to be visionary. What does that mean? To be visionary, one must have the ability to dream and imagine beyond the practical and to see things that others may not see. When a leader successfully imparts their vision into the minds of willing supporters, the dream has a way of coming to fruition. God himself said of the human race, "Behold, they are one people and they have all one language; and this is only the beginning of what they will do, and now nothing they have imagined they can do will be impossible for them" (Genesis 11:6, Amplified Bible).

Where there is vision and unity, nothing is impossible. God is visionary. He imagined the finished universe before he spoke it into existence, and ever since then, he has described his plan in great detail so that his followers can catch the vision of his eternal kingdom, and in unity with him, bring it into full expression. The Scriptures say in Revelation 22:17, "The Spirit and the bride say, 'Come!'" because in the last days the Spirit and the bride are unified in vision and pursuit.

We must allow the vision of his kingdom to become large in our minds because we will not stand in faith for something we cannot perceive; this is why the Spirit of God is working tirelessly to cure spiritual blindness in the body of Christ. A preacher cannot show something to his congregation that has not been revealed to him.

Many of our "Institutions of Higher Learning" train their students in the art of proclaiming, but not so much in developing the ability to *see* by the Spirit, so the church in a general sense, has had a limited view of God and has preached a limited redemption.

The prophets of old were called seers because of their ability to *see* into the mysteries of God,

Therefore, the function of a prophet is first of all to *see,* and then, to *proclaim.* If the voice of the prophet is silenced, the advancement of the kingdom is greatly hindered.

Of the gifts of our Father to the church in Romans 12, the gifts of Jesus Christ to his church in Ephesians 4, and the gifts of the Holy Spirit to the church in 1 Corinthians 12, there is only one that is common to all three listings—prophecy!

Prophecy is composed of two inseparable elements: forth telling and foretelling. To reject the predictive nature of prophesy is to invalidate the declarative function as well. To accept the forth telling element of prophesy is to accept its predictive nature also; God never authorized anyone in his church to accept only half of a word's meaning or purpose.

The gift of prophecy functions every time a minister preaches the gospel message, and so every messenger of God has a responsibility to be open to the predictive nature of that same gift. God may very well desire to speak his vision to that congregation.

Unwavering Faith

People waver only when trying to focus on two opposing viewpoints simultaneously. So the solution is simple: *look only at one of them!*

> But let him ask in faith, with no doubting, for he who doubts is like a wave of the sea driven and tossed by the wind. For let not that man suppose that he will receive anything from the Lord; he is a double-minded man, unstable in all his ways.
>
> James 1:6–8 (NKJV)

Though the context of this passage refers to asking God for wisdom, the concept here is presented to us as universal: faith-filled people do not waver. Doubting people are unstable and aren't able to receive *anything* from God.

When we focus entirely on the covenantal word of God, faith rises and doubt begins to wane, but if we look at the practical impossibility of a given situation, doubt storms to the forefront and ultimately gives way to fear.

I heard Phil Pringle once said, "The heart is the believing machine and cannot be occupied with two major issues at once. Don't try to believe in your heart, while harboring unforgiveness." Focusing on the word of God *and* unforgiveness, or the *facts,* or any other sin or distraction, will result in *wavering.* We are not nearly as good at multi-tasking as we would like to believe for one simple reason; it is impossible to give

100 percent of our attention to multiple things. As the number of things vying for our attention increases, the amount of attention given to each one, decreases. This is usually how the things of God become less influential in a person's life. I heard Joseph Garlington once said, "If the devil can't make you bad, he'll make you busy." Busyness doesn't always indicate productivity; sometimes, it produces instability. The human being was initially designed to be occupied with one central thing; the kingdom of God, and when we put him first, everything else will find its place of fulfillment. It's not our job to *be* God, it is our job to *serve* him!

So as we fill our hearts with his Word, faith will rise, enabling us to *see* and *grasp* the power of God. We will speak it forth authoritatively and cause his kingdom to come, and his will to be done on earth, as it is in heaven.